IS HEAVEN
Really
FOR
REAL?

IS HEAVEN Really FOR REAL?

... What are the Odds?

JERRY NELSON, Ph.D.

JERRY NELSON MUSIC
PRESS

Is Heaven Really For Real?
© 2021 by Jerry Nelson

Every attempt has been made to credit the sources of copyrighted material used in this book. If any such acknowledgement has been inadvertently omitted or miscredited, receipt of such information would be appreciated.

Edited by Tracy Fagan of Kingdom Publishing
Cover design by Brad Nelson

For bulk orders, please contact us at www.JerryNelsonMusic,com.

ISBN 978-0-578-81058-4 (paperback)
ISBN 978-0-578-81059-1 (ebook)

Names: Nelson, Gerald O., author.
Title: Is Heaven really for real? : what are the odds? / by Jerry Nelson, PhD.
Description: First trade paperback original edition. | Denver [Colorado] : Jerry Nelson Music, 2021. | Also published as an ebook. | Index included. | Bibliography included.
Identifiers: ISBN 978-0-578-81058-4
Subjects: LCSH: Heaven—Christianity. | Angels—Christianity. | Miracles—Anecdotes. BISAC: RELIGION / Christian Living / Inspirational. | PHILOSOPHY / Religious.
Classification: LCC BT846.3 2021 | DDC 133.9013 NELSON–dc22

"What a refreshing approach: Time-honored truths in 'real life' terms without offending skeptics or believers. Jerry's opening stories implying a *relational* God are fascinating. Each chapter presents fresh, new insights. An inspiring read!"

Steve Adams
Author, Composer

"Jerry Nelson didn't just recently decide to write a book on heaven. It's been 50 years in the making. Jerry is the gold standard of integrity. Read this book with confidence and great joy."

Dr James Diehl
General Superintendent Emeritus,
Church of the Nazarene

"Jerry's stories reminded me of 'Five-Minute Windows' in my own life I had forgotten about. The book made me realize it was God's hand at work – not just amazing coincidences. The stories resonate whatever religious biases a person may have."

Jon Burchfield
Nashville Recording Artist

"Jerry Nelson produces here a harmoniously blended collection of heart-warming stories. The anecdotes are encouraging, uplifting, and faith-producing. In all ways, a persuasive reminder of God's blessings."

Dick Etulain
Historical Writer, Professor Emeritus of History

"Do you believe in miracles? If you do you will be inspired by Jerry Nelson's new book and you'll find yourself reflecting on the miracles in your own life. If you don't, I challenge you to read this book and hopefully, prayerfully you will come to know the God of miracles."

Johnny Hall
Director, One Voice Mission
Colorado Springs, CO

CONTENTS

Acknowledgements

How do I properly recognize the many who have given either a nod of encouragement, wisdom, opinion or challenge as they've perused this manuscript? I'll take the risk of citing just a few: Steve Adams, Jon Burchfield, Susan Caudill, Roger Clay, Johnny Hall, Roy Hanschke, Scott Nelson, Phil Nelson, Tim Stearman, Ken Tippitt and Jim Van Hook.

Publishing, these days, calls for the arms of an octopus stretching in all directions as we explore the multiplicity of marketing options, potentially including direct print, thumb-drives, tablet readers, audio books and a music recording with its variety of playback media. We have been blessed to tap into the counsel of Tracy Fagan, of Kingdom Publishing, whose experience as a publisher, editor and advisor, has been incredibly indispensable in steering us through the maze of options.

My son, Scott, had his fingerprints in the production and mixdown of much of the recording, "Is Heaven Really For Real?" which provides a valuable musical companion to this book. Brad, my younger son, is always an encourager and adds his expertise not only in marketing but you're seeing his professional touch in the design and layout of these recorded and printed products.

Colton Burpo, at age 4, was the subject of "Heaven Is For Real," a book authored by his father Todd (now in 24 languages). Along with the movie, it has touched an estimated 35 to 40 million people with its phenomenal story. For literally months, and whether a 'brief' 2-hour phone call or sitting across a table in the mountains, their shared "heaven" nuggets, advice and encouragement can't possibly be exaggerated.

Dr. James Diehl ("Jim") has been a first-name-basis friend for decades having served with him on a church staff and enjoyed hearing more than a myriad of stories spun from a wealth of life experiences. His willingness to add his true story to my collection, will affirm, for many, the reality of "Angels" and, by implication, the reality of a place called "Heaven."

Most of all, I have been blessed with a phenomenal wife who, despite all of the challenges in her busy world (including her multiple roles in over 1,000 of my concerts) has endured my persistence and interruptions. She has lent her incredible wisdom, advice, insights, marketing experience and untiring commitment to another one of my brainstorms. That calls for an unbelievably loving wife – a role only Rachel could fill.

Dr. Jerry Nelson

A portion of the proceeds from this book will be applied to our mission and humanitarian efforts in Rwanda and DRC Congo, Africa
World Wide Connections.

To learn more about this organization or to support them directly, please visit WWConnections.org

CHAPTER ONE

Is Heaven Really for Real?

A few years ago, a new book was released which took the country by storm.[1] By the time the movie had run its course, the hope of Heaven had been shared with an unprecedented audience of 35 to 40 million.

Could this intense interest in the subject of Heaven be attributed simply to curiosity? Millions are *more* than curious out of fear for their final destiny. That's why their numbers sky-rocket with every national crisis – unfortunately, so do suicide numbers.

Titanica –

This subject got me thinking back to an orchestral piece I wrote called "Titanica," featuring a spectacular, spacious, new ocean vessel.[2] The ship's paint was barely dry, when it launched on its maiden voyage from England to New York. The various instruments in my dramatic musical piece, for 16 minutes, trace the voyage of the safest, largest, most magnificent, most luxurious ship in the world. In print, the famous ocean liner was touted as "the ship that not even God could sink," even if <u>four</u> of its 16 compartments should somehow be ripped wide open. The details of this historic voyage are both fascinating and tragic.[3]

So confident was the crew (perhaps also in some denial) that - even after six stern warnings - the ship was allowed to speed through the fog and a maze of icebergs at a blazing 23 knots per hour. So confident were the ship's lookouts that they inadvertently left their binoculars back in Southampton. Preferring uninterrupted passenger views, the ship's lifeboats, by design, accommodated less than half of the passengers. None of the 2,224 on board could have dreamed that a brush with an iceberg before midnight April 14, 1912 would tear open *five* compartments.

Some seven miles over the horizon, The *Californian* had sent out 'growler' ice warnings to the Titanic that had seemed ignored. Now, in the distance, its crew curiously watched Titanic's lights slowly disappear (as if mired in quicksand.) Californian's wireless operator – weary of a string of weather transmissions off the Newfoundland Coast, and weary of being ignored – had impatiently disregarded Titanic's frantic SOS pleas for help and casually shut down for the night. Just ten minutes later, the doom of the historic Titanic was sealed.

After an hour, with all lifeboats now adrift and its bow slowly sinking, many of the stranded passengers scrambled back to the rails of the stern. Many, in denial, still assumed *Titanic* was "unsinkable." Others had already declined the biting cold of a lifeboat seat preferring, instead, the warmth of their cabins.

Their denials left 472 lifeboat seats vacant! Two hours after its fatal fault, the great ship could no longer handle the stress.

With a ghastly shuddering sound the immense ocean liner shredded down the middle into two massive segments. The unimaginable forces created by the sinking bow hoisted the stern vertically like a giant, 250-foot, leaning tower etched against the star-studded sky. There it hung suspended for almost 60 forever seconds, as if surveying its ultimate destiny. Finally ripping loose of the bow, it torpedoed 2 ½ miles down in its 5-minute plunge burrowing a 49-foot crater deep in the unforgiving, silent, ocean floor. Unbelievably, more than 1,500 of the midnight voyagers were swallowed up in the icy waters of the Atlantic. Only 705 survived.

None of them could have imagined how soon their life's journey would come to a screeching halt. Many might have already pondered the question "Is Heaven really for real?" Others might have wished they could, even last minute, have plowed through the pages of a book like this to help decide which side of the question they land on. Given their awareness that this ship would soon be on the ocean floor, some undoubtedly were wondering if, in fact, there is a heaven and, more importantly, how do I get there.

The Most Challenging Line to Write –

It was the top line on this book's cover. Before going to press, we bounced around three options: "Is God Really for Real?" … or "Are Angels Really for Real?" … or "Is Heaven Really for Real?"

The first option is pivotal. But I thought back on Titanic's last couple of hours. I doubt that the frantic chatter rose to such a high, lofty level as the first question poses. As for option two, some may have been praying desperately for an angel of rescue but found none on the horizon. The last option, "Is Heaven Really for Real?" had a ring of urgency. It's where the rubber meets the road. No question could have been more crucial in that moment.

Those on board the Titanic, I expect, had varying perspectives on what was about to transpire. As they stared helplessly over the rail, I suspect there were some very heavy dialogues going on. Some were quite solidly convinced that if this ship goes down, in the grand scheme of things, it's not really a big deal; it's simply the *end* of it all. There is no forever.

Others, however, had lived their lives with hope and expectancy. For them, Heaven would be just the *beginning* of "forever." So I pose the life changing question, "Is Heaven *really* for real?" That is our focus.

Can the Question Even be Answered? –

I would like to think that it can. Most people would agree that if Heaven is for real, it stands to reason there would have to be a *supernatural being* and not simply in the sense of a Creator-being.

To create a place which offers his creation an eternal destiny, this supernatural being must be one who chooses to intervene in the lives of those He has created. One who would identify with their pain and struggle; and whose intervention in their lives is very intentional, purposeful and very obvious to those who receive it.

Chapters 2 through 10 consist of several very interesting vignettes – drawn from my journal of more than 100 stories that, statistically, are so extremely improbable they suggest the strong likelihood of a supernatural power intervening in the details of my life. Some readers prefer to play the role of "Devil's Advocate," (D.A.) for the sake of debate. It helps them sort through the issues that separate contrasting positions. If you are playing the role of a D.A., these stories offer you a chance to challenge the laws of probability.

What gives these stories such extreme improbability odds is the fact that, repeatedly, the events occur within narrow "Five-Minute Windows," creating, exponentially, even stronger odds.

While these are rather astonishing stories, they don't, by themselves, offer absolute proof that there is a supernatural being, or a "God." However, the chapters which follow provide, progressively, greater challenges to a D.A.

What's your category? As a reader of this book, you fall into one of three categories. 1) You may be convinced there is no such supernatural being and, consequently, no Heaven. You would consider yourself an Athiest. 2) You may be quite confident that there is such a being whom we may identify as "God." Or, 3) you are uncertain and, quite possibly, on a search to know, for sure, the answers to these most provocative questions.

Debate on a Level Playing Field –

Wouldn't it be fun to hear the extreme positions debated by two persons equally qualified to defend their systems of belief? In fact, there *was* such a recent, landmark debate in which an intelligent Christian spokesman and a highly respected Atheist took the platform in front of 8,000 very focused listeners and more than 100 radio stations. After two hours of moderated debate, the audience would vote on which belief system was the most compelling. In a later chapter, I will share with you the results of that vote and the historic debate.

As one who identifies with the second category above, my challenge, in this book, will be defending an entire domino chain of assumptions: My belief in God, Jesus Christ, the Resurrection and Heaven. I call it a domino chain because if even one domino falls, the whole chain goes down in which case, Heaven might just as well be fantasy-land.

A final precaution – It is possible that you or I, while defending *any* belief system, could be so locked in that no amount of evidence will persuade or dissuade. It was an Atheist who offered this very striking insight which I would ask you to remember. "Christians believe because they *want to* and Atheists don't believe because they *don't want to.*"[4]

This insightful observation raises a yellow caution flag for both Atheists and Christians or advocates of *any* stripe. We are inclined to believe what we *choose* to believe, so we yield to the temptation to use every bit of evidence to prop up our *choice*. Instead, we should be tenaciously pursuing TRUTH, even if the evidence compels a change of heart or mind.

With that admonition, we charge into the remainder of this book. Wherever you are in your adventure, I think you'll find this a fascinating, all-consuming journey.

Quik Stop – CHAPTER ONE

Each chapter will be followed by a Quik Stop. One or more questions posed may each have one answer, no answer or several answers. They may prompt you for your opinion or your belief. They may ask for recall of an idea or fact you just read. Or, they may ask you, on a scale of 1 to 10 "How compelling or believable was this chapter for you?"

- Some believe, in regard to the Titanic tragedy, that a British newspaper headline was actually prophetic; in fact, almost predictable. (I can understand God being angry). What did that headline read?

- How many, to the nearest 100, were lost in this disaster? How many survived?

- Many passengers had to be thinking about eternity and Heaven that night. What would your final thoughts have been while staring helplessly over the rail?

- Do you believe in angels? In Heaven?

- Where do most of your beliefs originate? Family tradition? Peer pressure? Reading material?

- Who were among the "notables" that died? Who survived? [See the Chapter 1 Notes at end of book.]

- What is your reason for reading this book? Some interesting stories? You are on an honest search for answers? You enjoy playing the D.A. role, challenging opposing views?

- When you *choose* to embrace a belief, do you find it easy to change that belief in the face of evidence or do you find yourself quite locked in?

C H A P T E R   T W O

Angel in Greasy Overalls

D ecember 31, 1960 in St. Paul, Minnesota, was a crisp
night. No. Minus 15 degrees and dipping lower is *not*
what you call "crisp." *"Bitter"* was a more apt description, as
we packed our three cars to caravan back to college in Nampa,
Idaho, after two weeks of braving another sub-zero Christmas
break. And like every night that week, this night, also, was "too
cold for a junkyard dog."

Darkness had just set in - at 5 PM - as I walked down to the
local grocer for some last minute supplies before the long,
1,500-mile trek back to college. The ground audibly squeaked,
as I made my way back from the store. No, it wasn't my
heavily-padded Sorels. If you've experienced living in a
climate where the high temperatures for the week could be
minus 5 degrees (dipping down to minus 30 at night), you
would recognize the squeak of the snow underfoot with each
step you took.

As I returned from the store, walking closely past an empty
parked car, I recoiled spontaneously when the vehicle started
without warning or driver. Minnesotans use every trick in the
book to ensure a certain start in the morning, including dip-
stick heaters to prevent oil coagulation, wrap-around battery
blankets, frost plug heaters to keep the anti-freeze warm, and

remote starter devices at pre-set intervals through the night to help keep the engine starting.

Two weeks earlier, three rather dated cars had caravanned "home for Christmas" from Nampa, Idaho to St. Paul, Minnesota. The two weeks of vacation break were bitter cold…but not so much as to keep us from some ice skating or skiing in the gutters along country roads, towed by a long rope behind Dad's car. If you are the one on the skis, just remember to pull up some slack and flip the rope over the occasional country road signs. Timing is everything. Another sport involved speeding our cars down a hill on to a frozen lake to see who could perform the most 360's without taking out someone's fish house.

Sadly, however, now the fun was over. It was Dec. 31st and time to pack up for the long 2-lane trek on highway #2 across the frozen tundra that skirted the Canadian border. My brother

Phil and I, were both driving *Kaisers*: a brand which hadn't been manufactured in several years. Here's a shot of my Kaiser. (FYI – If you'll be stopping in Yellowstone, always roll up the windows and lock your car).

We could be almost certain that no stores supplied parts for 10- and 12-year old Kaisers. So with 19 passengers in three sedans (Go ahead and run the math on that one!), someone had to shoe-horn seven students into his sedan for the 38-hour marathon. Two nights and a day would get us on campus just in time for the required chapel service.

Fifteen of the passengers were girls, and four were guys. Not bad odds for the guys! How it was that Dad ever let us take off with two such high-risk vehicles is still beyond me. But when it's all the transportation you have, and you're young and ready for a lark, it's easy to overlook some of the risk factors that, ten years later, might have raised a big red flag bordering on a heart attack.

As the stream of passengers dropped by our house to make their contributions to the packing ceremony, everything one could imagine had to fit into three trunks. But we hadn't anticipated all the Christmas gifts that didn't make the trip East two weeks earlier. Besides the blankets and heavy winter gear, there were TV sets, desk lamps, audio speakers, and even a new trombone that couldn't be left behind. None of the three drivers solved the jigsaw puzzle of fitting every piece into his trunk. The solution: bungee cords and blankets to stop at least some of the bitter cold that would syphon in around the back seat.

The Long, Cold Trek –

By 8 PM we were headed North toward St. Cloud. That should put us in Fargo, North Dakota by 11PM. But 75 miles before Fargo, my Kaiser began to sputter just a bit. Ten miles later our speed diminished until 30 mph was all it could muster. And the trip was downhill from there. The rest of the caravan necessarily slowed down along with my car, as we chugged along...speculating on the likely mechanical failure. Thankfully, I had spent enough time under the hoods of old cars to have some idea whether the problem might be fuel-or-ignition-related. My first guess was the likelihood of a failing fuel pump.

We pulled into Fargo about two and one-half hours later than expected. Consider now the very remote possibility that a parts store would have had a Kaiser fuel pump sitting on the shelf. Add the fact that it was now 2 o'clock in the morning.

Moreover, this was New Year's Eve. Tomorrow would be New Year's day. It would be 30 hours before *any* store would be open.

Having spent many teen-age hours in salvage yards, I knew that finding one would be my only option. But while we would search for a used fuel pump, what would we do with 15 girls who couldn't afford so much as a Motel 6? We pulled into the first hotel in sight and, explaining our dilemma, begged to let the girls simply lounge in the hotel lobby for a few hours. Morning would set in soon. The all-night desk clerk graciously obliged.

Mind you, there were no cell phones in the 60's. Just phone booths with Yellow Pages. Through a process of "eenie-meanie-miney-mo," my finger landed on the only scrap yard on the page. We jumped into Phil's Kaiser and headed North to our destination. The game plan? Locate a Kaiser (Good luck!); remove a fuel pump; then send the proprietor a check the following week.

Arriving at "Bill's Best Buys," we jumped over the fence. Well, not quite. With three feet of hard, packed snow crusted on top, anyone could ride a bicycle over it. We found our way to the other side, with no fear of some dog's big bark or an even bigger bite. Like I said, the night was "too cold for a junkyard dog." We gazed out at acres of white bubbles. I guess we should have anticipated that. Like penguins in their tuxedos, every car looked identical. What was the ultra-slim chance that even one might be a Kaiser? What were the odds? Finding *any* specific car would be like rolling six snake eyes six times in succession; but expecting to find a *Kaiser* was decidedly like trying to find a needle-in-a-haystack (under 3 feet of snow).

By this time, I was really beginning to feel the anxiety that circumstances like these engender. Lacking any hope of salvaging a used part, I could see no option in sight. A part of me was almost despairing of the possibility, though I dared not admit it. Even if we waited until Jan. 2nd, we'd be starting at square one. We saw absolutely no answer...except pray. No fancy words. No "dear Father in Heaven Who created all that is...and Who alone is not only omnipotent but omniscient, Thou Who knowest all about us in our most distressing circumstances, wouldst Thou, in Thy great kindness...." No, it was more like "God, *help*! If ever I needed You, it's now! Pleeeeze, God. You've gotta pull a rabbit out of the hat! Aaaaa-men." Nothing pretty. Just short.

It took Phil and me less than *five minutes* to conclude that there was no possible way to find a Kaiser in this sea of white bubbles...and no possibility of future success in standing around a sea of frozen, junked vehicles at what was now 30 degrees below zero. We might as well join the party back at the hotel.

We headed back toward Phil's car, when a truck pulled up. What? This couldn't be! Why would *anyone* be pulling up to a salvage yard at two in the morning at 30 below? For anything whatsoever? (Maybe a "Five-Minute Window" coincidence?)

An Angel? In Greasy Overalls? –

A man stepped out of the truck. We murmured, "Oh no, he's wearing a badge." After very minimal small talk and a bit of dubious assurance that this was his salvage yard, he explained that he also doubled as the county sheriff. He asked if he could help in any way. We presented our somewhat scripted, though unrehearsed, dilemma, concluding with "What is the chance that you might have a 1951 Kaiser fuel pump on your shelf?" "Well, there'd be nothing like that on the *shelf*." ... a long pause .... "No guarantees, but it seems there may be a Kaiser way back in that corner!" He gestured in a far distant direction.

Then, handing us a shovel, he advised: "Best way to find one is...dig down through the snow to find a hood ornament. If you find one on a Kaiser, you're welcome to have at it."

We walked across the frozen tundra to the far corner of the lot and proceeded to dig down to one hood after the other. Often we had to bore two holes, since you couldn't tell a trunk from a hood.

Glancing back at where we'd entered, this unidentified man had simply disappeared. As quickly as he had appeared! No waiting for a payment. No instructions on how to pay or what to do with the shovel. He was simply gone. No white wings. No choir of nightingale voices. No flowing, white robe. Just a pair of greasy overalls.

But after a half hour, we struck something better than gold: a Kaiser hood ornament. Unbelievable! What model and year? Who cared? It'd probably fit!

We would have to access the pump from underneath the engine. No fun, since all the wheels had been removed. The undercarriage was frozen to the ground. We began shoveling a trench around the entire vehicle, eventually working a jack under the front bumper. With wrenches in hand, we rotated the job at 5-minute work intervals to avoid permanent frostbite. About 90 minutes later we finished what would normally be a 20-minute job: simply extracting the pump.

We still didn't know if a fuel pump *was* the problem...or if *this* fuel pump might *also* be failing.

We drove into town, somehow assured that this could be the night we'd witness a "rabbit out of the hat" spectacle. Then, begging an all-night service station for use of their hoist, we drove my Kaiser inside the garage to gain its toasty warmth; and I proceeded to replace the fuel pump.

Parenthetically, let me share a taste of my brother Phil's sense of humor. While I was installing the pump, he drove back to the hotel where he met Diane (my bride of just three months) and wove this partially-true saga: "Jerry and I sneaked over the fence of a salvage yard; and before we could even look for a fuel pump, the sheriff showed up and arrested him for trespassing and intent to steal. Since it's a holiday weekend, they won't be able to bring him to trial for 2 or 3 days." Poor Diane was in tears before he finally 'fessed up.

Consider what had to happen that Dec. 31st (which was now Jan 1st) - despite the date, the temperature, and time of night working against us:

- We had to correctly assess the cause of the problem.
- There had to be a Kaiser among the *acres* of salvaged vehicles.
- Though old and maybe a bit rusty, its fuel pump had to be *functional*.
- At much greater odds: we had to be standing at that fence line during a 2 AM sliver of time - no wider than 5 minutes - during which time a truck would pull up.

With a much used fuel pump in place, we headed down the highway at 60 mph. The whirr of my engine was like music to my ears, and no one had to be convinced that something extraordinary, and well beyond "happenstance," had occurred. An angel? That's what I'm thinking. We had 1,300 more miles to test that fuel pump, and it worked like a charm.

Any Angels in Montana? –

However, we had barely crossed the Montana line, when my engine developed what sounded like a rod-bearing knock (much more serious than a faulty fuel pump). It was now daylight when I stopped at a ranch where an engine mechanic resided. "Hey, we are 19 kids heading back to college; but I think my engine might have a problem," I explained. "Would you mind listening and giving me your honest opinion?" He lifted the hood and placed a sounding rod between his ear drum and the engine head. "Well, I hate to give ya the bad-ugly news. But ya asked for my honest opinion. I think ya done got a rod-bearing going out on ya."

Goodness! I knew what *that* meant: find a Kaiser *engine* somewhere! "Well sir, we have about 700 miles yet to go. How fast do we dare drive to spare that rod from going through the pan?" I asked.

"Well, I think I'd keep 'er under 35." We took his advice and drove the last 700 miles at half speed. It looked like we were in for a second sleepless night. In the bright of the full moon, we followed the river through West Yellowstone Park and were startled at the most amazing spectacle. Deep snows had driven the elk down into the valley. We estimated that between 2,000 and 3,000 elk were meandering across the highway for the next 3 or 4 miles, like herds of sheep without a shepherd. We slowed to a crawl, zig-zagging through the magnificent, shoulder-to-shoulder scene.

Every few minutes we'd feast our eyes on some of the biggest bull moose we'd ever seen, feeding along the river on the South side of the highway. I decided to have some fun. With absolutely no cars in sight for the last two hours, I drove over onto the *left* shoulder to just gawk at one of the biggest bulls I'd ever beheld in all my years of wandering the woods.

I sensed he was beginning to get nervous; and, not wanting to cross the river, he proceeded to trace a big arc *behind* me. In response, I shifted into reverse and cut him off. This time he drew a large arc in *front* of my car. In response, I shifted into low gear and headed him off once again. This little game continued for three or four more passes. At that point his nervous manner turned into agitation and ultimately belligerence. He put his head down and charged straight at my car from behind.

This brand of animal has been known to take on a bus. And *win*. Some of our readers would know that Kaiser clutches are a bit jerky and could easily leave a driver stalled. Not to worry. I used three times the normal acceleration, as I slipped the clutch and kicked rocks all over the highway in our escape.

Continuing on West, we enjoyed passing through the somewhat out-of-character, Craters-of-the-Moon and on through the fascinating town of Twin Falls... ultimately reaching our destination: Nampa, Idaho. The 35 mph speed proved good advice. We had circumvented the likelihood of a blown engine and could now proceed with having the rod-bearing replaced. After 52 continuous hours of heart-stopping, eventful excitement, we pulled in just in time for chapel (though on *Tuesday*...instead of *Monday*).

Come to think of it, I didn't see any of our gang in chapel. Come to think of it, if they were there, they didn't see *me*!

◻   ◻   ◻   ◻   ◻

In Retrospect –

In retrospect, those 50+ hours of adventure seemed to have inexplicable, if not, supernatural fingerprints all over them. Somehow we knew we were up a creek without a paddle. Now you may tend toward a bit of skepticism as I do. You may even question whether there is a God. That's OK. In fact, you may find yourself explaining away every providential detail of this story. Well frankly, I've never seen an angel myself. Or, if I did, I may have simply been oblivious of its presence which may have been the case in that Fargo salvage yard.

But the more I read about angels in the accounts of those with startling stories to tell, the more I'm thinking "there has to be a Mind interacting in the midst of my dilemmas" – a Someone, if you will, that is relational enough to not only *care* about my little crises, but also *do* something about them. And just maybe He is constantly dispatching Angels of Protection when his kids are in deep trouble. And if I'm on target, I doubt they are wearing wings. I've heard they are disguised in three-piece suits, police uniforms, blue jeans, tuxedos, greasy overalls, you name it.

It was this Kaiser adventure, as a college senior, that prompted me to start a journal that I call "All of His Benefits." Fifty-plus years later, that journal contains over 100 stories of the most improbable, most unlikely events that, for me, can only be explained by my circumstances intersecting with a hand of Providence that would seem to defy all odds.

It is my hope that, as you continue through these true stories, some of which are much more earth-shaking, life-and-death stories, you will recall similar interventions in your own journey. Perhaps it will prompt you to start your own journal. More important still, I hope the excitement of witnessing events that defy the laws of probability, will find you in a search to better understand the possibility of "providence" working in the *trivial* as well as the *crisis* events of *your* journey.

Quik Stop – C H A P T E R   T W O

- The idea of angels may still be new to you. On a scale of 1 to 10, how compelling and believable is this chapter? Why?

- If you have any understanding of the characteristics of angels, what features or behaviors of this midnight sheriff match such behaviors or characteristics?

- If this sheriff was, in fact, an angel, do you think he knew exactly *which* white bubble was a Kaiser? If so, might he have had good reason to withhold telling us its precise location?

- If an angel had not appeared at 2 AM, and, with only $200 in your pocket, what option might you have favored?
  - o   Wait 2 days and find a mechanic
  - o   Put 6 or 7 kids on a bus
  - o   Uber for 2600 miles round trip
  - o   Call Dad for wisdom (and a loan)
  - o   Locate a benevolent "brother" in Fargo, kind enough to drive 2600 miles for a "reasonable" price
  - o   Drag my Kaiser to Bill's salvage yard and hunt down an ugly but cheap and reliable Chevy.

C H A P T E R   T H R E E

Ambush at Galilee

A s a Junior High music teacher back in the 70s, during a summer break I linked up with a Gospel Quartet for 90 concerts in 90 days. My late wife, Diane, though inexperienced, had a very pleasant soprano voice and found a spot singing with the group.

As a pianist with no recording experience, I suddenly found myself recording with highly acclaimed orchestras and musicians from Atlanta and Nashville to Los Angeles and New York and making every mistake in the book. I also was discovering that arranging and recording music could be a lot of fun if I could only learn how to do it. Meanwhile, I was sure having a good time trying.

Recording Across the Pond –

Rubbing shoulders with others in that industry, I quickly learned I could save some serious dollars by taking projects overseas. London's magnificent city with four major orchestras seemed never to run out of musicians. Its players, at $7 per hour in the 70s, were half as much as state-side musicians. In calculating the cost to hire 30 players, the savings of going overseas quickly added up; even factoring in the cost of round-trip air fare and lodging for our US based team.

Casually chatting with Kurt Kaiser, then-President of Word Records, I learned that the musician rate with the *Israeli* Symphony was just $5 per hour. So our next recording trip, we attempted something rather unprecedented. We recorded rhythm and brass in London and then took the huge 2" tapes to Tel-Aviv to add the strings and a Rhodes electric piano. I had assumed all these years that audio recording standards were universal around the world. We quickly came to find out this isn't so. Fortunately, we were quickly able to locate one little screw which adjusted the pitch and brought us in sync with the London recordings. And we were off and running.

I was accompanied by my Producer, Ken Tippitt. How do we entertain ourselves on a 16-hour, trans-continental flight? Ken and I found a way. In my pocket was a pocket-metronome: a tempo-setting device looking much like your grandfather's pocket watch. Its long-sweeping, back-and-forth hand and tick-tock sound effect could be adjusted to any tempo. I would set an arbitrary tempo,  and Ken would see how close he could guess the set tempo. Then he would set the tempo, and I'd do the guessing. This interesting game went on for hours, until we landed in Tel-Aviv. In those days, large planes didn't pull up to the terminal. Instead - for security reasons - they parked out on the tarmac, while passengers boarded buses to the terminal. Everyone descended the stairs from the plane and, in single-file, boarded a bus. *Except for me*!

I've Been Profiled –

I was baffled and confused when an officer, at the bottom of the stairs, grabbed me by the arm and pulled me under the plane…where he proceeded to ask me a flurry of questions: What was my name? My length of stay? My employer? My destination? My purpose in coming? I hadn't experienced the "Spanish Inquisition" on any previous trips. After about five minutes, I was released (though perplexed by an inquiry involving *only me*).

Once settled in our hotel, we made our way out to the street to enjoy life in Tel-Aviv. Relishing the aromas and tastes of Israeli foods is part of the wonderful experience of recording in the Holy Land. Recording sessions in any foreign country also have a flavor that varies from one country to the next.

In the Tel-Aviv recording sessions there was the added challenge of dealing with a different language. While some of the musicians were well acquainted with English, most of them were not fluent enough to follow instructions in English. Therefore, hiring a translator was necessary.

As part of our international recording trips, Ken and I would always plan to rent a car and explore the country we were visiting. It was exciting to be able to visit destinations that are considered the most sacred soil in all the world. We'd visit Bethlehem and Jericho.

One of the more memorable sites overlooking the Dead Sea was Masada, a flat, natural plateau rising almost straight in the air, more than 1,000 feet high. King Herod had built two splendid retreat castles and a large fortress, where he and a thousand Israeli zealots could retreat.

Too Funny For Words – We've never stopped laughing about a very funny human interest story while revisiting Old Jerusalem – always a given stop. By then we had learned there are peddlers of everything imaginable in most any foreign country. Anyone who even slightly resembles an American is an easy target. I suggested to Ken, "If we spoke a different language, wouldn't that be the end of the sales pitch?" Ken agreed. So we both came up with our own unique, cryptic combination of syllables. Mine went something like this: "Mahaka dela goocha klein voochi mega svar": sort of a mix of Hawaiian, German, Italian and Russian. It had worked perfectly on a street corner in Athens. The peddler, there, just sauntered off with a puzzled expression (as if to say, "They sure *looked* like Americans.")

So we tried the gimmick on a narrow street in Old Jerusalem, when the larger crowds hadn't yet arrived. "Ken, see those two guys a block down? I think we're a target for buying some wooden camels." Continuing in their direction, about 75-feet before their shop, we went into our gobbl-de-gook jargon. Without a moment's hesitation, one gentleman looked me straight in the eye and remarked "Your pants are unzipped." Instinctively, I looked down at my zipper. I didn't have the cool or the time to consider my response. I had been had. No doubt about it. They made no effort to make a sale. They just laughed like there was no tomorrow. And so did we.

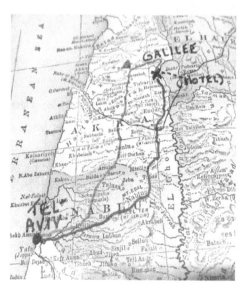

Our final night we usually spent in a little hotel on the West side of the Sea of Galilee. Come morning, we'd pack up and drive across the parking lot to enjoy a brief glance at the sun as it bounced its eternal rays off the Sea of Galilee. We'd then make a left turn, taking us North along the Sea, ultimately driving through Nazareth and on to the Tel-Aviv airport.

But this particular morning was different. We sat at the parking lot stop sign enjoying a five-minute view of the sunrise. It dawned on me that if we turned right, and took an alternate route, we might see some scenery not previously experienced. Whipping out a map we charted our course, made a right turn, and proceeded *south* to the airport.

Arriving at Tel-Aviv airport two hours early, we sensed an eeriness in the air. Perhaps it was because of the Israeli soldiers armed with M16 assault rifles at all outside corners of the terminal. Perhaps it was the increased number of armed security guards inside. Perhaps it was the process of spreading all eight of our 2" recording tapes across the table and opening every box. Maybe it was the officer who removed everything from our suitcases, deftly feeling the liners for the slightest hint of a hazardous object. One officer was spraying every deodorant can, while another agent pulled the screws from our hair dryers, totally dismantling them for inspection.

The Inquisition Begins –

Unlike previous trips, this time airport administrators had assigned *three* security officers to the *two* of us for extensive interrogation. We were immediately separated and taken to separate little booths where the process began. Removing half of our attire, we were forced to field questions while officer #3 functioned as a runner - between our two booths - who corroborated our responses for consistency.

This arduous security check went on for almost two hours until boarding time. The possibility of Ken and I not making our plane began to set in. Meanwhile, security officials continued to ask me cryptic questions. I tried not to betray my anxiety, but I eventually realized that we were 20 minutes past departure time. When I mentioned this to the attention of my final interrogator, he calmly responded, "We'll let you know when we're done."

About this time, the reason for the very special, thorough treatment we'd been receiving finally dawned on me. It had to be that metronome. It didn't occur to me, at the start, that the flight attendant would find that strange, ticking object to be highly suspect. No doubt she immediately reported the incident to the captain, who notified ground security. Then, from the moment we left the plane, Ken and I had been profiled. Apparently I'd been holding the device when the flight attendant walked by and noticed the ticking. Quite possibly our whereabouts were tracked for the entire duration of our stay. At the very least, they knew the date, time, and flight number of our departure.

Thirty minutes after scheduled lift off, after all buses had delivered their passengers to the plane, I was assigned to a private car which hustled me to the boarding ramp. As I entered the aircraft, the gazes from the passengers were not pleasant ones. At that moment I didn't care. I was never so happy to board a plane. Exceedingly grateful they'd delayed it a half hour - just for me! I guess I should have felt like a celebrity; but I did *not*.

Ambush and Massacre –

The plane finally landed in Rome, our planned destination for the night. The next morning we picked up an English-reading newspaper. On the top of the front page was a map of Israel, pinpointing a spot near the location where we had stayed the previous night. Quickly scanning the printed article, I was stunned to discover that around 9:15 AM, during the 5 minute window of perusing our map for an alternate route -

insurgents, coming down from Lebanon in the North, were ambushing every car on the route we were planning to take through Nazareth. They methodically gunned everyone down. Dozens were massacred along our intended route that morning.

If there ever was a time when I doubted the existence of angels enveloping us with protection, I no longer had reason to do so! Heaven's angels may not have been visible, but I'm inclined to believe they made their presence known at the stop sign by the sea and once again by delaying the plane until we both boarded.

If you're looking for an angel, don't look for wings. I believe that celestial beings can make an appearance in casual vacation attire, sport coats, and greasy overalls. Maybe that's why we "entertain angels unaware."

If there were, in fact, angels at the scene, it would provide confirmation that Heaven is for real. Without Heaven there would be no angels. If this story is not adequate evidence of angels, keep reading. There is, perhaps, more convincing evidence ahead.

You'll recall our hotel departure coinciding with the ambush en route to Nazareth. And you recall those five minutes we sat at the hotel parking lot remapping our route to Tel Aviv airport. Just another one of those "Five-Minute Windows" that defy all odds.

Quik Stop – C H A P T E R   T H R E E

- Where did the narrow "Five-Minute Window" occur in this story?

- In those "Five-Minute Windows," some people tell of having heard an audible voice. My need to turn right at that stop sign was critical. Think of a time you experienced when you heard a small voice or had that internal prompting to make a correction burn.

- When might an inaudible voice be more effective than an audible voice?

- On a scale of 1 to 10, how compelling or believable is this story as it relates to angels and Heaven?

- Life-saving crises often happen on road trips and vacations. Can you recall one or several?

C H A P T E R   F O U R

The Platte River Mystery - What are the Odds?

I love numbers and probability theory even though I'm no math wizard. Maybe it's the influence of those four intense Statistic courses I took during grad school. Whatever the reason, I'm fascinated by any scenario that defies statistical odds. The "Platte River Mystery" is not as consequential as the other stories in this book. However, if you're at all skeptical, you have to admit these odds are over-the-top staggering.

To keep you from experiencing a graduate level statistics course, I want to offer this simple illustration to increase your appreciation for how 'odds' play into the stories in this book. We will look at four variations of a simple roll of the dice.

What Are The Odds? –

Let's say that each morning you roll three dice onto the breakfast table.

Game #1: Roll any three identical numbers (111 or 222, etc.). Roll just once each day, and it should take you about a month to roll three identical numbers.

Game #2: You must roll three of any <u>predetermined number</u> such as 444. Odds are, rolling once each day: it would take you about half a year to roll 444. Is this getting fun?

Game #3: Same as Game #1, but you want *any* three identical numbers (example – 111 or 222, etc.) on <u>two days in a row</u>. You're maybe thinking, this would double the required number of days. But no. Statistically, it will require the better part of a Decade.

Game #4: Same as Game #2 but requiring the <u>same</u> three numbers (444) <u>two days in a row</u>. You'll have time for game #4…but not until you get to heaven, where time doesn't exist. Statistically, it will take more than a quarter of a millennium or over 250 years!)

When you add the element of "repetition" (two days in a row), you experience what I call "Exponential probability" which often calls for "divine intervention." Keep this factor in mind, as you read the next few chapters.

One day I was reading a bit of advice the Psalmist David had written in the book of Psalms in The Bible. His admonition was simple: "Don't forget all of His benefits" (Psalm 103:2 *NIV*). Putting his pen where his mouth was, David started journaling some of those benefits: The odds of slaying a giant (Goliath) two or three feet taller than he. The odds of doing it with a slingshot. The unlikelihood of surviving the swing of Goliath's sword which was longer than David was tall. The improbability of defeating an army many times the size of his own.

Miraculously, David survived all four of the above challenges. Any one of them would justify writing home about. But the odds of pulling off all four *in one setting* are extremely improbable. That's what we call "Exponential Improbability."

You've just read about the Psalmist David as a young boy. Later in this chapter, you'll read about "King" David – considered the greatest King in Israel's illustrious history. Yes, it's the same David who relied on His God throughout a lifetime. What a legacy. We shouldn't be surprised that Jesus was born from the lineage of this same shepherd-King David.

David journaled partly for personal reasons, so he wouldn't forget the awesome things that he and his predecessors had witnessed: events that defied all odds. But he also said, "This will be written for the generation to come, [so] that a people yet to be created may praise the Lord" (Psalm 102:18 *NASB*). Little did he know that 3,000 years later, THIS generation would be dramatically affected by his journaling.

David's admonition to chronicle those events in my own life that seemingly defy all odds, is what got me started on my own personal journal. At about age 30, I combed through a decade of previous history to recall past events that were so improbable that the only explanation could be, in a word, "Providence."

The Platte River Mystery –

"The Platte River Mystery" is one such story which was "exponentially improbable." Consider the monumental odds in this story!

Over the years we had hired a painter by the name of Francisco to help us keep up with paint maintenance on our studio in the Rockies. One week my wife, Rachel and I were preparing to leave for concerts in Branson, Missouri. It was a perfect time to get some painting done at our home in Denver. We knew we could trust Francisco's meticulous skills with brush in hand. Better yet, we could trust him with the keys to our house.

Just one problem. In a city of two million people, we had no idea how to reach Francisco. He could not afford email or a computer. We didn't know if he even owned a cell phone. We had no idea what side of town he might be living on (if, in fact, he was still in Denver at all). We knew he could use the work, because he had previously mentioned needing money to return to Mexico to care for his ailing Mother. We were just one day away from departure and probably didn't even venture so much as a prayer toward locating him, since our starting odds would be 1 in 2,000,000.

The day before we were to leave, I was driving 20 miles across town to find a rare wheel that I needed in order to repair a trailer I had borrowed. I was crossing the Platte River but stalled in mid-bridge, waiting on a long stream of traffic at a red light. I may have been car number 25 or 30 in the line-up. Impatiently twiddling my thumbs, I was running out of time. Casually, I glanced out the passenger window. What, to my wondering eyes did appear...but Francisco. Was this a coincidence or what? He had been hired for just one day to help finish painting the bridge; and this was the day!

I quickly engaged him in conversation. "Francisco, I need to get the interior of our home painted. Can you help?" "When would you need me?" he asked. I responded, "Like, tomorrow...if you can." I whipped off a note with my address and phone number, and that was as good as a handshake.

As I drove away from that scene, my mind did hand-springs, trying to comprehend all the factors that had to intersect to pull this needle out of the haystack. Besides the population odds of 1 to 2,000,000, someone had to:

1. link us up on the very same day;
2. come up with a good reason for me to drive across town;
3. route me across that particular bridge of The Platte; and

4. do so on the *only* day Francisco would be working the bridge. But consider this *very* slim probability:

5. I could easily have been stopped 10 cars, or even 10 feet, up the line and totally missed Francisco standing just three feet from my window. It gets down to *feet* and *inches.*

6. I just "happened" to glance to my right. Are you thinking "exponentially?" Then, consider that:

7. Francisco "just happened" to be taking a one-minute break at that brief moment. You see it even gets down to *seconds.*

8. For no particular reason he was facing up-stream – away from the railing he was painting – and thus looking straight into my passenger window.

The likelihood of connecting with Francisco for a two-minute conversation that day is astronomically unimaginable. To top it all off, I had been lamenting having a run-in with a curb which had bent the wheel I was trying to locate. I was still kicking myself for having to take the time to deal with the situation. But had that little accident not occurred, I would never have been on the Platte River Bridge at all.

I'm not into astrology and planet alignment. I would seldom even use the term "luck" in any context. And certainly not now. But think with me; as I drove away, my mind was processing the unlikelihood of what I had just experienced. Somehow, I could imagine God up in the ionosphere, with elbows leaning on the balcony of heaven, looking down and thinking, "Jerry's gotta connect with Francisco somehow. I know a thousand ways to make it happen, but watch his eyes pop when he sees Francisco in the middle of this bridge gazing right into his passenger window!" And 'pop' they did.

The nature of the eight improbabilities I've shared above is such that no one can arrive at anything close to the mathematical odds of their actualization. Just consider the "coincidence" of #4, #5, #7 and #8 all converging at once. Who knows? It may be in the billions.

The Laws of Probability –

We tend to think about "miracles" as events that defy "the laws of physics." But miracles can also defy "the laws of *probability*." A skeptic might reason, "Hey, the Platte mystery is no different than winning the lottery. *Someone* has to win." But what are the odds the winner would ever win it twice? One would immediately suspect some insider of manipulating the drawing. That's where "exponential" probability enters the equation.

You see, my journal now has more than 100 stories of such interventions. And many of the stories are of much greater consequence than this one. "The Platte River Mystery" is just one of many "Five-Minute Windows" that defy all odds." Maybe I *do* have an "Insider" manipulating my odds.

Lest you think my faith is all about numbers and probabilities, let me assure you of this: Just as the Biblical King David's faith was buoyed and reinforced by thinking back on occurrences he experienced in bygone days, I find recalling my own supernatural Platte River memories to be especially significant during those times when I might be inclined to question or doubt if I'm going it alone.

For many of my readers, the thought of miracles defying "the laws of probability" is very real and well beyond simply theory. Others find such a concept quite remote if not impossible. Whatever your stance, it's quite OK. It may well be an idea that's never crossed your mind.

Quik Stop – C H A P T E R   F O U R

- What odds do you think come closest to explaining this incident? 1 in a thousand? 1 in 2 million? 1 in 20 million? 1 in a billion?

- "Miracles" defy the laws of physics. How could Francisco's unexplained appearance on this bridge be an example of a miracle defying the laws of statistical improbability?

- Since Francisco was an acquaintance of mine, is he ruled out as a likely "angel"? If so, did God have anything to do with his off-the-charts appearance at that very moment?

- What law of probability might be in play in order for this miraculous connection to occur?

- On a scale of 1 to 10, in terms of statistical improbability, how compelling is this story?

CHAPTER   FIVE

Challenging the Mountain

I n 1973 Diane and I along with our boys, Scott and Brad, moved to Denver to direct an orchestra in a thriving church. We purchased a home in the city, but I wasn't particularly a city guy. I loved the outdoors. I enjoyed hunting, though more often than not, I would end up sitting on a high rock writing music. (My comrades oft reminded me of my propensity to fall asleep with elk wandering casually in front of my closed eyes.)

Life on Conifer Mountain –

Immediately, on moving to Colorado, we all fell in love with the mountains. Soon we discovered a lot on a rock ridge at the peak of Conifer Mountain. Its view encompassed Pikes Peak, 65 miles to the South. To the West was a stretch of the Continental Divide. To the North was Long's Peak towering above Estes Park, and to the East you could see half-way to Kansas. The vast panorama encompassed some 12,000 square miles of majestic mountain vistas.

Colorado Mountain High – Of course, "Eagles Nest" would have to include a full view of Pikes Peak and the million dancing night lights of Denver, 5,000 feet below. It was in this environment that a flurry of inspirational music projects would blossom over the next 25 years.

The dream of a *home* somehow evolved into a *recording studio* and escalated further into a 5,500 sq. ft. *studio / retreat* facility for 18 or 20 aspiring musicians at a time. Funny how dreams have a way of mushrooming the budget to where it necessarily becomes a little-by-little, do-it-yourself project. The venture would take years, not months. Hiring a crew to construct the shell, my boys and I, assisted at times by wonderful friends, spent four years bringing the rest of the dream to fruition.

At that time, in the mountains, building codes were more tolerant of do-it-yourselfers. A major impetus was the fact that my father was a carpenter. Beyond that, we sought the counsel of professionals at our church – like Art Dockum, coaching us in plumbing and heating, and electrician, Mike Bauer who, one very late night, drove 80 miles to get a furnace going. Dick Robertson, husband of my secretary, Barb, was our architect.

For readers who enjoy this kind of stuff: we also figured out how to install an in-wall vacuum system, a hot tub, tile floors, counter-tops, solar collectors, cabinets, and oak fireplace mantels. I will admit, taking on five baths and 2 ½ kitchens was a huge bite for us novices. But designing and building the recording studio with double-stud walls and thick, acoustic, sound-barrier doors – well, that was more like fun than work.

But the most fun was building decks. They're more forgiving. Limited only by our imaginations, we kept dreaming up one deck after another to add to the diversion.

I have to say that no other project we've ever embarked on forged more family bonds and pure gratification as Eagles Nest – not simply as a building project but for the years of creative adventures that emerged as we worked side by side.

Eagles Nest – the Studio –   If you turn to the back cover photo of Eagles Nest, the studio is located behind the prow-shaped windows on second floor. "A studio surrounded by glass?" you ask. Unusual, for sure. However, on a ridge atop a 10,000-foot mountain, it was uniquely situated up where elk roam and the world is whisper quiet. Open the windows for a gentle cross-breeze and take in the view of Pikes Peak. For a musician, nothing could be more exhilarating.

Recording 400 voices at 10,000 feet – Eagles Nest was an incredible environment that gave birth to a host of recorded projects. Scott enjoyed his role as engineer in this setting that was about as close to heaven as one could get. Brad was the art designer for each recorded project.

The most ambitious venture, logistically, was recording a complete project with our 400-voice Rocky Mountain Praise Choir. Sound impossible? Not really. First we set up headphones for 100 throughout the pool room, library and studio for proper isolation. We recorded four separate 5-hour sessions with 100 singers per session, eventually layering them together in mixdown and post-production. Included in the repertoire were some of the best of Broadway. We recorded with windows wide open. The next day, neighbors down the mountainside inquired about, what sounded like, a massive choir singing "The hills are alive with the sound of music."

A project of the scope of Eagles Nest - on the rocky ridge of a mountain - wasn't without a multitude of challenges and risks. There are numerous stories we could tell but here are some of most memorable ones.

Record Snowfall – Three-and-four-foot snowfalls were not unusual on the mountain. But none of us can forget when *our* record was set. Scott, was up at Eagles Nest mixing a recording project, all alone, when it began snowing. It was a heavy, spring snowfall that wouldn't quit. After two continuous days, it had accumulated 7-feet on the level. The drifts on the driveway were much deeper. The county plows wouldn't reach the mountain top for five or six days.

The deck on the South side always got the brunt of a wind funnel effect that typically left almost twice the amount of snow. Despite the towering snowdrifts, Scott would start his day in the hot tub off the South deck. The snow on that deck, now at 13-feet deep, totally blocked his view of Pikes Peak and covered half of the second floor windows.

The third morning, he awoke and headed for the hot tub. Amazingly, Pikes Peak was suddenly in view again. He reasoned, "the snow couldn't have settled that much overnight." He was right. In fact, the snow's weight, calculated at 30,000 pounds, equivalent to eight normal-sized sedans, was too much for the deck, causing it to cave in and slide down the rocks. What a great time to have a bunch of eager-to-help musician-friends! A few days later, about ten of them joined us in rebuilding the deck.

Meanwhile, however, Scott had another challenge. With government plows still working the highway as well as the roads near the bottom of the mountain, our son had exhausted his supply of emergency groceries. He was helpless; *until* it dawned on my sister, Sonja - on a neighboring peak a half mile away - that she had *two* pair of snow shoes. She could snow-shoe up to the studio and bring along the second set for Scott. This was her delight since her husband, Dean, was on a work assignment on the other side of the world. Scott snow-shoed back to their house, where he spent the last couple of days before a rescue plow arrived.

A Target for Lightning – At Eagles Nest's 10,000-foot altitude, we were the natural target of lightning strikes. I remember, as if it were yesterday, when a spectacular bolt of lightning struck the earth just 25-feet from the kitchen deck, igniting a blinding fireball about 5-feet in diameter. It hung suspended above the ground for a few seconds before quickly shrinking into nothingness.

Sometime later, it was necessary to pull one of the lightning rods out of the ground to pour a concrete pad. Unfortunately, I failed to replace that rod immediately – a fact that dawned on me later as 18 guest retreaters were moving in. That night while gazing out at a flurry of spectacular lightning displays, a fork of lightning blasted the temporarily unprotected portion of the Eagles Nest roof and lit up the insides with such intensity, it blinded our eyes for several seconds. The surge made its way through the house… knocking out the big-screen TV, the 24-track recorder, numerous digital light switches, and more.

Six-hundred feet up the driveway, the surge blasted open the thick steel door on the breaker-switch box and blew the interior panel across the road, ripping out all six retainer screws in the process. "OK God, I'm impressed!"

The next morning, I climbed the roof to find two 8" holes burned entirely through the roofing and all the way through the 3/4" plywood underlayment. Reaching through the fire-charred holes, I grabbed handfuls of insulation. With its shake shingle roofing, it is, without doubt, a miracle that Eagles Nest didn't burn to the ground. A volunteer fire department would likely not have arrived in time to spare the facility.

That major hit prompted me to restore the third lightning rod in the ground (after which we experienced no more hits on the place). I became a believer in angels. If, in fact, an angel presence was on duty that night, it would affirm that "Heaven is *really* for real" – because that's where angels come from.

The Roofing Incident – Our very steep roof was 30-feet up at its peak and 22-feet from the roof's edge to the concrete below. I had traded my production work to a man in the roofing business. One day I was on the peak of the roof, carefully standing with one foot on each side of the peak. Our roofer-friend was standing near me…but not at the very peak.

Down below, along the edge of the roof, he had installed a 2 x 4 cleat to catch hammers and tools that might have a mind of their own. He was usually tied off with a safety rope, but at this moment, he wasn't wearing one. With both feet on the same side of the roof, he lost footing and began a rapid skid down the roof. He immediately knew enough to go down feet first into a spread-eagle posture during his frightening skid.

I was helpless to do anything but offer a very short two-point prayer. First of all, that he wouldn't go into a tumble and fall 22-feet to *the concrete apron*. Secondly, that *the 2 x 4 cleat* would support his weight, if he was blessed to hit it just right. *Both* prayers were answered. He bounced off of the cleat, stood to his feet, and walked somewhat more cautiously to the peak. While pointing to the life-saving cleat, the first words out of his mouth were, "Well, that's why I put it there."

Potentially "career-ending" – My father wasn't just a carpenter. I guess I latched onto his "do-it-yourself" mentality. And, yes, I made probably more than my share of mistakes while learning the hard way. I have to confess, I didn't always "measure twice, cut once." Dad also taught me everything I needed to know about power tool safety. Even so, with the nearest hospital being 30 miles away in Denver, it was wise *not* to work alone.

But much of the time, as on one particular day, I *necessarily* worked by myself. No neighbors even close by. Nearing the end of our four-year project, I was cutting some oak trim using a miter saw with a big 10 ½ -inch blade. I was cutting just one inch off the left end of a 12-foot long board. Typically, a right-hander would hold the board with the left hand and use the right hand to bring down the blade. But holding the stubby, one-inch end with *either* hand would be risky. The logical option would be to "reverse hands."

But obviously, without thinking, I "crossed hands" so that my left hand was now under my right hand. With my right hand I brought that huge blade down. Instantly I heard a "zing" typically indicating the presence of a nail. "But this was a *new* board," I reasoned. Removing the board, I rotated it in my hands searching for a nail.

No nail was found. But, while rotating the board, I noticed where that huge blade, in less than a microsecond, had sliced half-way   through my watch missing my wrist by 1/4 inch.   You   may know that when a limb is severed with any   power   saw, one's   body   shock system   delays   the 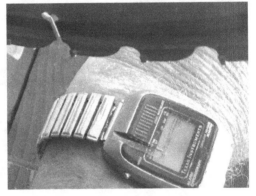 response so that the pain isn't immediate. It's just too late. (Notice the huge 10½ inch blade just above the watch!)

If my watch had been on the *right* hand where I often wear it, my hand would most likely have been severed. Could this have been a "career" game-changer? No. More likely a "home"-changer. And Heaven would be that home. What would be the chance of surviving a 30-mile drive into Denver without passing out or bleeding to death? Likely an angel on the scene?

There are more pleasant stories to tell. Suffice it to say, however, that if this experience taught me anything, it was to embrace the full meaning of the familiar Scripture, "He will give His angels charge concerning you to guard you in all of your [careless] ways" (Psalm 91:11 *NASB*).

My son, Scott, was the chief engineer at Eagles Nest Studio situated at 10,000 feet atop Colorado's Conifer Mountain.

My son, Brad, the graphic artist in the family, adds his polished touch to each of our projects including this book and accompanying music recording

Yes, leaving Eagles Nest behind was a bit of bittersweet. But it was never really ours. It was God's gift to us as well as many friends and colleagues for a season. That season is now behind us ... but the best is yet to come...And Eagles Nest won't compare!

Quik Stop – C H A P T E R   F I V E

- Incidents like in Chapter Two are fairly isolated. But the risks working on a mountain (weather, power tools, tall ladders) are rather daily and on-going. They incline me to believe in a permanently assigned Angel of Rescue. What are your thoughts on this idea?

- As a young kid, I recall darting full bore through a stop sign on my bike and missing the city bus by just a foot. On another occasion, working underneath my car when the jacks gave way and the car compressed every bit of oxygen from my lungs. Again, I have to think a rescue angel bailed me out. What "rescues" of this sort can you recall from your own experience?

- If you recalled such rescues, were you a person of "faith" when they occurred?

- Do you feel such angel-interventions occur only with people of faith, or also non-believers?

- If they occur with non-believers, what message might God be trying to get across?

CHAPTER   SIX

Peace in the Valley

H ave you noticed how much deeper you breathe when your job feels secure; health is perfect; and all of life seems to be coming together? But we've all experienced what it feels like to face inexplicable losses, heartache, and insecurity. The pink slip on our desk…or the intonation in the doctor's voice, as he presents a picture of what those X-rays suggest and struggles for words that might soften the blow.

For better or worse, loss is a part of life. It's something we all experience at some time or another. I felt it, when I lost my wife, Diane, to cancer. I was crushed when a trusted friend deceived us, stealing one-third of our retirement. When the national economy did a one-eighty, leaving me with minimal financial security, another one-third of my savings was stripped away. The loss was extremely painful, to say the least.

Rachel and I were about to leave one Saturday morning for Sunday concerts in Durango, Colorado. The trip would take all day, so we needed a 9AM getaway. As she was filling our drinking containers for the trip, she remarked, "Jerry, there seems to be hardly any water pressure at the kitchen sink. Just a dribble."

That was strange. We get our water from the city at 60 psi, and that hasn't changed in 35 years. I made my way to the basement, where all utilities originate. When I opened the basement door, I immediately noticed the carpet was all wet. Actually, there was a layer of mud and a puddle of water covering the entire basement carpet. This puddle was *four and one-half feet deep* and getting deeper by the minute. Very soon it would be creeping up the walls on the main floor. I had to move swiftly.

Trouble In River City –

My heart naturally sank. I was totally overwhelmed by what I saw. I was afraid to step into the ice cold water, for it had climbed half way up the stairs. I would have to swim the length of the house and then claw my way through the mud to reach the main shut-off valve in the far corner of the basement crawl space. At that moment my only thought was, "I have to find a way to stop the flow of water." The cause of the problem wasn't important right then. We could cross that bridge later.

Then it dawned on me that I had a means for stopping the water. *That very week* I was in the hardware store, walking down the rows of plumbing parts and tools, when my eyes fell on a three-foot long fork like those that cities use to turn off water pressure to any house. This gadget, when inserted into a six-inch manhole could completely shut off the water pressure with one simple turn. When I saw that wrench in the hardware store, it occurred to me that I hadn't ever had a need for such a tool in 35 years. But it might come in handy sometime; and for just a very small investment, I'd have it hanging on my pegboard. So I purchased it. How could I have known I would need that wrench in a matter of days or hours?!

What had caused the water in my basement? And when? It seems a large PVC sprinkler line coupler - underground, just a foot outside the house - had severed after 35 years of use; and the full volume of water was entering full blast through an access hole in the foundation. Taking mud along with it! I had been in the basement - before turning in - just eight hours previously, and there'd been *no* problem. The water had risen to 4 ½ feet in this part of our basement in just 4 to 5 hours. Going unnoticed for 2 to 3 more hours, the water would be in the main level living quarters. Being a split-level home, it would take in the living room, my office and studio, the family room, utility room and hot-tub room.

Being Saturday morning, there is some question whether the city water department could even be summoned for a trip out to our house in time to avert an even worse disaster.

My Life's Work Under Water –

We lost the entire basement: all the walls I had built and paneled and the carpet I had laid, plus the furnace and hot water heater. It was deemed a *total loss*. Though the damage was to the home's interior, because the severed pipe was one foot outside the house there wasn't a dime of insurance coverage. We fought the ruling vigorously, but in vain.

Perhaps the greatest loss was the contents of six drawers of filing cabinets consisting of 35,000 pages of hand-written music manuscripts. This essentially represented my life's work up until a few years prior. It was then that I began writing music using a computer and storing everything on hard drives.

It's easy to get philosophical at a time like that and ask the "why" questions. "Why me?" "Why now?" *But in that moment,* despite a certain level of frustration while trying to leave town, I must tell you that *there was a settled peace* which I couldn't muster up on my own. Rachel, in fact, voiced her surprise at how calmly I responded to a major crisis and simply went methodically about the task of dealing with the problem.

When I shared this crisis with my son, Brad, he came up with his own philosophical analysis. He said, "Dad, I think I know why this happened to you." Immediately, my ears perked up, wanting to hear what wisdom might come from a son 30 years younger than I. He went on, "I think it happened to give you another illustration to use in your concerts." Oh, thanks Brad. There are other ways to come up with interesting illustrations. Just a little of his typical sense of humor coming out. And about that time I probably needed it.

The Silver Lining –

This domino of unfortunate mishaps isn't really so much about the losses. I've long-since recovered from the financial hit and forgotten about its magnitude. I've managed to survive without the 35,000 pages for the past 15 years. I've learned once again that even in the worst of life's vicissitudes and struggles, I can see the hand of God moving and "all things working for good."

1. Looking for "that silver lining," I found two wonderful reasons to rejoice...despite considerable loss:
   I've already shared the very unusual "coincidence" of purchasing a wrench I thought I would likely never need only to discover I'd need it before the week was over.
2. A much greater reason for rejoicing might have totally eluded me. Follow this logic, because it is not pure speculation; it is precisely what would have happened.

If this pipe had severed just eight hours later, we would have been on our way to Durango. Not even our nearest neighbor, could have known what was about to transpire. In just four hours, three-fourths of our home would have been engulfed by the rising flood waters. As the level would have naturally progressed up the walls, the slight gaps around the doors could not come close to accepting the volume of water at the rate it was gushing from the pipe. Within 6 to 7 hours, the water level and resulting water pressure against the window panes would have burst the glass. Quite possibly the neighbors would finally have realized that our entire house had become a swimming pool. They would not have had a clue where we had gone…or for how long.

This story encourages me to look for the silver lining behind *every* cloud that comes into my world. Hopefully, it encourages *you*, as well, to see the hand of God in the middle of life's storms.

And, who knows? Perhaps there is an angel dispatched on a 24-7 contract to protect Jerry and Rachel from unimaginable crises like this one. Perhaps you have one also protecting you.

Another "Five-Minute Window."

Putting the finishing touches on one of the 35,000 hand-written pages, all of which were destroyed in that flood. The next 15,000 have been written and stored on computer!

Quik Stop – C H A P T E R S I X

- Unlike the high-risk, rescue situations cited, probably the majority of times I see God's hand in the critical <u>timing</u> of events. Chapters 2, 3, 4, 6, 7, 8, 9 all look through ultra-slim "five-minute windows that simply defy all odds." These are the often overlooked episodes.

- What narrow timing windows can you recall that strongly suggest a hand of providence?

- Does your life, or that of your family, seem to call for an *occasional* angel or a *full-time* angel?

- What "catastrophe" can you recall from your own life's experience? What silver lining did you discover in the process which reminded you that "God causes everything to work together for the good of those who love God and are called according to his purpose for them" (Romans 8:28, *NLT*)?

- Do you have some souvenir or momento (like this emergency wrench hanging on my pegboard) to help remind you occasionally of being spared of a catastrophe? When you get to Chapter 10, you'll see how someone else has made use of a reminder as common as a stick pulled out of the river.

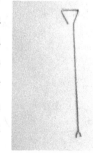

CHAPTER   SEVEN

Angel in the Jungle

Ever since we were married, Rachel and I have both had a heart for Africa. In 2006 we were invited by Tom and Ethel Lowry, retired Africa missionaries, to join them in three weeks of mission ventures that would take us to Zambia, Malawi and the Democratic Republic of the Congo. That was the first in a series of Africa trips.

Rachel's zeal for Africa along with her awesome gifts of organization and genuine passion, was the catalyst for an Africa trip which we hosted in 2008. We promoted the trip in our local church, Denver First Church though the word apparently fanned out beyond those borders. It wasn't long before we had 35 friends and acquaintances signed up to join us in a two-week adventure that, like an octopus, had its fingers out in all directions.

This mission venture involved a number of different projects including the first phase of a new church building, a children's ministry, discipleship training, a music evangelism team, a medical team, a dental team, a team focusing on the AIDS pandemic in Africa and a team dedicated to establishing economical water filtration systems for even the smallest families. It soon became clear to Lanny York, our missions pastor, and Rachel, who was spear-heading the entire effort, that we had probably taken on too many projects. But she valiantly pressed on, holding the many threads together.

We had all met at our church the morning of departure to pack a large trailer with 77 bags which included medical and dental supplies, water filters, two musical keyboards, sound systems and all of the personal bags for each person. A non-stop flight took us from Denver to London, with a connection in Harare, Zimbabwe. The final leg of this forever journey, landed us at our primary destination, Lubumbashi, DRC Congo.

The Luggage Debacle –

We all waited patiently as the many bags of luggage were unloaded to the conveyor belt out on the tarmac of Lubumbashi airport. It was easy to identify each bag of luggage as it came down the belt. But when the last bag had left the plane, it was clear that a number of our bags were missing. In fact, at final count, only six of the 77 bags had arrived! It was at great length and after pursuing answers to many questions, that we were told the reason most of our luggage did not come through. The Congo only provides fuel for its own planes. Since we were on Ethiopian Air, in an effort to lighten the load, they must choose between more luggage vs. full fuel tanks to accommodate the next leg of flight. The latter was certainly a wise choice.

For the next eight or ten days, we had a new missions team: "The Luggage Team" which went to the airport every morning and sat through the unloading of every incoming plane. It was absolutely essential to view every piece coming down the belt knowing how common it was for baggage handlers to hide cargo in a back room, only to "discover" it when they saw some twenty-dollar bills coming their way. Bribery is a way of life in Africa and especially in their profession.

One piece of luggage didn't arrive during our stay in the DRC ultimately ending up in Amsterdam. The remaining 71 missing pieces trickled in, though most of our medical and dental supplies and keyboards didn't arrive until just days before the group was to go home. In the United States one could expect to receive some compensation for luggage delayed to that extent. Despite every question and effort in that direction, it became clear that we could not expect even a dime of compensation.

But back behind the curtain, a different drama was about to unfold. It would be just another one of those incredible "Five-Minute Windows" defying all odds. Somehow we made good use of every effort and we learned that these precious African people needed our hearts more than they needed all of the tools, supplies and stuff we would leave behind when we headed home.

When everyone had boarded the plane for their return, Rachel and I stayed on for another ten days or so, teaching and performing concerts in Zimbabwe. We teamed up with two American friends who met us en route for ministry in Zimbabwe. Les and Lane Thomsen are the founders of a very thriving Zimbabwe ministry, "Noah's Farm". Rachel continued her teaching on the subject of AIDS while I worked with their musicians making a joyful noise to the Lord. While there was much we felt we could teach them musically, there was so much we needed to learn from them as we listened to the pulsation of their rhythms, the richness of their deep voices and watched them dance and move, driven by the passion of their hearts in genuine worship.

Victoria Falls is over one-mile wide. Truly one of the Seven Natural Wonders of the World, sharing its border with Zimbabwe and Zambia.

Hippos by the Hundreds.

Fun camping with the wild animals, along the mighty Zambezi!

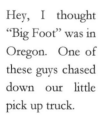

Hey, I thought "Big Foot" was in Oregon. One of these guys chased down our little pick up truck.

Mana Pools Safari –

After several days, we asked if there was a way we could take in an African Safari, but without the typical and expensive guided safari with proper attire, narrator-host, hotel and the typical vehicle that encages tourists for maximum security. Both Rachel and I enjoy a fairly high level of risk. We asked "could you, instead, line us up where we could maybe have our own open-air pickup? And how about shelter sort of out in the jungle, maybe in a tent instead of a cabin or hotel? Really, we'd like to be closer to nature if that is possible."

Sure enough, we were introduced to two friends of the Thomsens who offered to drive their two pick-up trucks, outdoor tents, cooking facilities and enough food for five days in the jungle. Moreover, they would agree to do all of the cooking. We've enjoyed some of the most awesome experiences in our trips to different parts of God's marvelous creation. But none has been as memorable as these five days. Each morning we'd jump in the pickup and head down a jungle trail. When we saw giraffes, zebras, elephants, herds of water buffalo, we would park the vehicle and head in their direction, being careful to heed warnings to avoid proximity to the most dangerous species.

This game park called "Mana Pools" meant Five Pools or lakes. Each pool was loaded with hundreds of crocodiles and hippos. After an outdoor breakfast beside one of the pools, Rachel grabbed a chair and wandered out on a little peninsula projecting out toward the center of the pool. Our guides kindly but quickly, and with hushed impatience in their voices, insisted she immediately get back to safety. She didn't realize what a target she could be for crocodiles who can move up to 12 mph in less than a second.

At night our tents were surrounded by monkeys, hyenas and wart hogs while hippos, after dark, would saunter out of the mighty Zambezi River just fifty feet from our tents.

Our final day, we engaged the only ranger in the park to help us find some of the big cats. We drove to a remote area and, at his instructions we moved cautiously in single file through the jungle on foot. Buzzards circling overhead told him we were likely getting close to a lion kill. Sure enough, within 5 or 10 more minutes, we heard the monkeys chattering their warning signs that lions were close by. Suddenly the warden, properly armed, stretched out his hand with a quick "Stop. Don't move even a little bit." Less than 50 yards away, was a pride of six lions licking their chops after feasting on a kill. It had to be one of our best photo ops.

Still hungry? Or just feeding the family?

Les Thomsen and Jerry ... Looking for the big cats.

Next we jumped into a pick-up and headed to the far East end of the jungle where a small river was dumping into the Zambezi. The river was making its small contribution to the enormous Victoria Falls which, 250 miles downstream, would pour as much as two million gallons of water per second over its one-mile expanse during the rainy season. Since the little stream prevented us from driving any farther, we jumped out of the back of the pickup to get a closer look.

We noticed a man with his son doing some fly fishing. He introduced himself as Bob Adams. We hadn't seen a white man in days, so I asked him if the fish were biting. He responded in perfect English. I asked him where he hailed from. "Idaho" was his response. It took no time to learn that he had flown on the same plane out of Denver that we were on two weeks earlier. In fact, he recalled sitting on the plane in the middle of our cluster of Africa-bound volunteers.

Just imagine. We left Denver on the same plane. Arrived in Africa in two different countries separated by almost a thousand miles, only to meet at the far end of the most remote jungle one could expect to find, visited only by African Nationals. Who, but God, constantly creating coincidence after coincidence, could have brought us together in such an incredibly improbable fashion?

The Five-Minute Window –

But that's not the end of the story. We were just about to experience one more of those "Five-Minute Windows." In the next five minutes of discussion, we learned that they not only had lost their luggage but had pursued an office in Zimbabwe where they received full compensation for their lost luggage that was ultimately returned.

When Rachel got back home, she contacted that office and the person whom Bob Adams had recommended. The bottom line? We received over $3,000 in returned funds from the airline and, as a group, agreed to send all of the funds to help with various mission projects in the Congo." I'm left to wonder, could this have been just one more angel sent by God, half way around the world, to open another of those "Five-Minute Windows" that absolutely defy all odds?

World Wide Connections

Our *non-profit* is funded by donors contributing to efforts such as our micro-financing program. It has helped hundreds of single moms leave the streets and start a productive business they and their children can be proud of. More than 144 ladies have grown their own businesses, and as members of their co-op, are helping other women begin their own enterprises. They now own this thriving business center in Rwanda.

Another of several WWC partner projects is the development of Fish Farms. This indoor Micro-Farm is used for production and training.

Our son, Blake, is equipping and training many youth to develop their own fish farms like this one. These farms will provide Rwandans with an affordable protein source and decrease dependence on costly imported frozen fish from China.

Quik Stop – C H A P T E R   S E V E N

- Sometimes we fail to receive the expected salary bonanzas and financial *gains* when, in fact, God's benefits often come in the form of *sparing* us from *losses*, such as hospital bills and expensive car repairs or learning a do-it-yourself repair.   Or, maybe providentially being introduced to the person who could *save* us hundreds of dollars.

- What situations of this sort can you recall when you were spared of painful financial loss?

- On a scale of 1 to 10, how compelling or believable is this true story?

- Might God have possibly slated us and this Idaho acquaintance to fly on the same Denver flight so that our brief conversation in a remote Africa jungle would quickly get around to the lost luggage issue?

- God could have connected us with this Bob Adams in any other setting: An airport terminal while headed home; a grocery store in Zimbabwe. But looking over the balcony of Heaven and orchestrating our meeting in one of the remotest jungles of Africa, is an irony of the most extreme sort. Do the remote, miniscule odds of this connection somehow do more for your faith than if we had met in downtown Harare, Zimbabwe?

C H A P T E R   E I G H T

London On A Dime

I 've often been asked why I travel thousands of miles to Europe to record my music. Aren't the players in the U.S. just as good? The answer is a resounding "Yes." But there are two big reasons for making the trek overseas. One is financial. For decades the musician rates have been lower in Europe. The larger the recording orchestra, the more advantageous is the overseas option. One day of recording with 25 or 30 players more than offsets the cost of airfare to a city like London.

The second reason is the number of players from which to choose. If recording in most any other city, one has to be sure to pick dates when other producers and arrangers aren't recording in the same area in order to avoid competition for the best players. London, on the other hand, has a plethora of orchestral players that is virtually inexhaustible. Where most major cities are blessed to have one professional, concert orchestra, London has four.

Performing great musical works with incredible performers is a breathtaking experience for any player or conductor. But for this cast of players, as exciting as these experiences may be, after several decades, many players begin to tire of the pace. Many opt for a more leisurely pace with less travel (thereby being less bound by rigorous rehearsal and performance schedules). One of the attractive options, especially for the cream-of-the-crop players, is doing studio recording sessions for many producers like myself.

To London Without a Passport –

I had no idea, when I left Minneapolis on my London flight, that I would be looking through another one of those "Five-minute Windows that Defy all Odds." Up before the crack of dawn, I was in the air by 8 AM. The flight had a three-hour layover in Detroit. But as I approached Detroit, while perusing my travel documents, I couldn't find my passport. Without a passport, no one boards an overseas flight.

I had scheduled these sessions a month earlier with studio, engineer, musician contractor and thirty players. My wallet was stuffed with several thousand dollars in the day's currency value. The players would be paid in U.S. dollars, CASH. Please understand: I couldn't simply call the musician contractor and cancel with the explanation that I'd forgotten my passport. I knew I stood to lose it all. What could I do? Might Diane pull my passport from the drawer in the basement and get it on the next flight bound for Detroit? That seemed to be my only chance. I quickly checked the flight schedule. The plane would leave in an hour and land in Detroit about twenty minutes before the London leg. At the ticketing desk, I explained my dilemma. The airline personnel were extremely cooperative.

This event took place before we had cell phones. In the middle of the Detroit departure concourse was a pod of four public pay phones. I appeared to be the only passenger in the area at that time. The place was virtually empty. Each phone booth had a small seat, a book of yellow pages, and a little ledge for writing notes. I deposited a dime to call Diane. She had left the house and was apparently out shopping. Since I was calling collect, my dime would return; and I could use it for the next call. It was placed to her Mother. That was a futile call. Diane's mother had no driver's license.

I called my brother-in-law, Norman. Thankfully, he was at work. I explained to him my dilemma and really gave him no choice but to become involved. "Norm, I need you to rush to my home, break into the basement window and locate my passport in Drawer #3. Then I need you to race to the airport, find a flight attendant for United Flight #2308, and - on hands and knees - beg her to hand-deliver the passport to me in Detroit." Norm happily obliged.

In between calls, an airline employee made a couple of trips to my booth to offer helpful suggestions on accelerating delivery of my passport. As I dialed several numbers, everything crept along in slow motion, like a snail caught in rush hour. Finally - having exhausted all possible options - the airline ticketing agent went back to his desk.

London – Without a Wallet, Driver's License, Cash or ID –

That was the first time that I noticed that my wallet was no longer on its little ledge. I knew immediately what had happened. This "helpful" airline employee was waiting for the slender moment when he could exercise his slight-of-hand. Suddenly I was left without a wallet, without a passport, without any ID, without a driver's license, and without the stash of hundred dollar bills that was to pay for the recording sessions. All I had left was a thin dime. And still I had no assurance that I could even board the plane!

With my heart beating a mile a minute and knowing exactly who had heisted my wallet, I scrambled to the ticketing desk.

Describing the bald-headed culprit, I expressed a need to see the man immediately. The response, "Oh him? It appears he needed to leave work early today."

This was one of those situations where, in just a matter of minutes, you feel so totally drained, you are unable to even think.

So, I did the only thing I could do; wait! Then wait some more…with a deep-seated hope that the plane with my passport would arrive on time. Where I'd go from there, only God knew.

Well, the Minneapolis to Detroit flight landed with my passport! Just in time to allow me to board the London flight!

For the next six hours there was nothing I could do but pray. I felt drained, helpless, empty, defeated, and broke. Arriving in London, that thin dime wouldn't buy a taxi, or a subway into the city, much less pay for a hotel. In Minneapolis I might have prayed for a familiar face from whom I could borrow a few dollars. But I have never, in all my international travels, met anyone I recognized in a foreign city, much less in London.

The plane landed at London's Heathrow airport. I sauntered into the terminal and plopped down in the nearest seat to think through my options. Casually watching the string of weary midnight travelers disembark, a middle-aged man caught my eye. He looked strangely familiar. Finally, it dawned on me. I had seen him on stage when the Spurrlows performed in Minneapolis. I wasn't totally sure but it seemed he was a brass player with the band. The name Stan jumped magically from my memory bank. As he made his way down the concourse, I followed him to make sure this wasn't just another look-alike.

Five-Minute Window-What are the Odds?–

I tapped him on the shoulder and quickly got past the hellos, "How's your Mother and your dog" before satisfying my curiosity. "Is your name Stan?" "Yeah, Stan Morse" he replied." I asked about his reason for coming to London. Amazingly, he was there on a mission similar to mine: Directing recording sessions for Thurlow Spurr. "Stan, I know this is a strange question, but I am wondering if you have a few thousand dollars you could loan a stranger? I will have my wife transfer money to your account before you get back home."

Well, Stan graciously understood my plight and was happy to loan the money. I don't recall how he planned to cover for his own sessions, but somehow he found a way to make it work. Diane wired the funds back to his account, and all was well. Clearly, there was much more at stake than in some of my other stories, but that's not the real issue. I, once again, connected with the Supernatural. He was there. Right on schedule!

"Happenstance" or "Providence." The odds are such that I have to believe it was Providence. Again, I am flabbergasted that I am personally in touch with the Sovereign, Almighty, all-knowing God of the Universe, Who knows me personally. The Psalm-writer, David, in one of his more eloquent and poetic moments, broke it down into the most minuscule events when he spoke of a God who knows when I'll sit or stand; He knows what I'm going to say before I say it. If I travel to the ends of the earth or even to London, He is there. I can't escape His watchful eye. And, honestly, why would I choose to? (Psalm 139 – my paraphrase).

He knows when I board a plane, when I'll forget an important document, when I only have a dime in my pocket. He even knows when, in the flurry of attempts to solve my problems, I lose my shirt. He's there. And once again in a "Five-minute Window," while plopped on a chair in a remote London concourse, He came up with a solution to my very critical need. And, in the process, his solution defied all possible odds.

How many times has He performed His connectional magic just for me? Besides the London airport, there was that salvage yard in Fargo at 2 AM – and again on a Denver Platte River bridge. Amazingly he showed up in the remotest Africa jungle 8,000 miles away – and again after a piano tuning in Minneapolis that changed the course of my career forever! And all of these within 5-minute windows!

My Cyberspace GPS –

A military specialist sat on a hill outside of Las Vegas while observing and manipulating a drone.   When the crosshairs lined up with his target, he pulled the trigger. In just microseconds, a missile was launched which wiped out a convoy of enemy vehicles 9,000 miles away in Afghanistan.

We are amazed at how GPS can connect two moving targets anywhere on this globe. Now imagine a gigantic GPS network manipulating a complex web of 7 billion moving targets, so that each target can pair up with another in microseconds. There is such a computer in cyberspace.

In fact, the God who created all 7 billion of us is capable of linking any person with any other on any side of this world, just as He linked me with Stan Morse in a London airport. Let me share an example in which He connected me with a total stranger 12,000 miles away. And He did it by opening, not one but *three,* against-the-odds, "Five-Minute Windows!!"

The New Guinea Connection –

Paul was a singer in the island country of New Guinea, reputed for its tribes of head-hunters. Paul had dreamed of making recordings to reach these primitive people with a message of hope. Take a peek through these three windows.

Window #1: – While browsing through a magazine, Paul was intrigued by an ad for a music conference in Estes Park, Colorado. Acting on a hunch, he bought a ticket to Denver. With no idea where Estes Park was, he took a bus into the city. While dining in Denver's iconic Larimer Square, he crossed the street to chat with jazz guitarist, Clyde Hankins.

Window #2: – Clyde was on a 5-minute break – just long enough to learn of Paul's dream and direct him to an Estes Park bus. Clyde was also a guitarist at my church and aware of my recording experience. Not having any contact information, he simply jotted my name on a scrap of paper and urged Paul to try to connect with a Jerry Nelson while in Colorado. Get ready for the next narrow window.

Window #3: – Ironically, Clyde had no idea that I had a booth set up at this Estes Park music conference to acquaint visitors with our production capability. Buying some time before the concert, Paul wandered down the rows of booths, eventually stopping at our booth and popping on a pair of headphones. While listening to some sample recordings, he noticed my name tag. His eyes lit up with a glint of amazement as he reached into his pocket and pulled out a crumpled piece of paper.

"Are you the Jerry Nelson that knows a jazz guitarist down on Larimer Square?" he inquired. "I think God sent me from the other side of the world to connect with you."

Long story short, we put him up for a few days. While he helped build a treehouse for our kids, we talked record biz. Wanting to see the East Coast, he hopped a bus with ear buds and a thousand sound tracks on "cassettes" to aid in selecting titles for recording when he returned. Before heading home to New Guinea, he recorded the first *two* of several projects with us.

The Muppet Show Connection –

I never tire of hearing of dot-to-dot GPS connections much like the scenarios I've been describing. The myriad of stories could go on all night. But let me share just one more.

Mark was a total stranger to me. An imaginative composer tucked way up where Washington shakes hands with British Columbia. Mark needed to link up with a fluid keyboardist-pianist, with strong background in arranging and 'improv'; specifically in a myriad of styles from Jazz and Blues to Gospel to Classical to Celtic. Also someone with skills in writing music on the computer and digital recording. A fairly tall order, given the small number of people fitting that description. The field narrows quickly when he also requested someone experienced in the Gospel-Christian market.

Mark had heard some of the music created by the Muppet Show producer. Attempting to reach him through the internet, Mark was unsuccessful since the man had passed away. But his music seemed tailored to Mark's needs, but with the possible chance of a "missing link" - the Gospel-Christian connection.

God must have chuckled at Mark's attempt to reach a Muppet Show guy coincidentally named *Jerry Nelson!!* Pursuing this identical name, Mark just "happened" onto *our* website. Just as providence had designed. I'm humbled that God, through a half-century of creating, had equipped me with the skills needed to satisfy Mark's need – including the missing link.

But beyond that, I too have to chuckle at the uncanny way that Providence came into play. The unlikelihood of two arranger-producers with identical skills in a career field with such a narrow band width of qualifications is rather mind-boggling in itself. But add to that the coincidence of identical names. What are the odds?

Long story short, it was just this week, while putting this book's final draft to bed, that Mark and I completed our first collaboration on his best original song

□   □   □   □   □

This concept of imaginatively linking strangers with strangers in such a purposeful design, totally fascinates me. It speaks so loudly of the *relational God* I've come to know personally!

Quik Stop – C H A P T E R   E I G H T

- Do you believe 1) Stan was an angel put on that plane by God, or 2) God simply engineered identical flight schedules and destinations, or 3) meeting Stan was a total "coincidence?" There was no *providential* plan. Why?

- If Stan might have been an angel, would you be more inclined to believe there is a "Heaven?" Why or why not?

- Considering the possibility of God being a real, *relational* Being, how compelling or believable have you found these three stories to be – on a scale of 1 to 10?

- Reflecting on my amazing connections with Paul and Mark, what jaw-dropping link-ups have occurred in your world? Pause and think. They may start to seep back into your memory bank. Could this be a good time to start your own journal? I've called mine "All of His benefits," inspired by a verse from Psalm 103, "Don't forget all of His benefits."

C H A P T E R   N I N E

You Just Can't Make these Things Up

For I know the plans I have for you," declares the LORD, *"plans to prosper you and not to harm you, plans to give you hope and a future."*
Jeremiah 29:11 *NIV*

D id you ever work a job that clearly was not a good fit? My first music career was teaching Junior High "Music Appreciation." Clearly this career challenge was not my niche; and, down deep, I think I knew it. But I was at a loss as to what direction to turn.

I grew up in a tiny church of 40 to 50 people, where, at age ten, I was designated the pianist: a position I held for 23 years. No one else in the church knew where "middle C" was! Oh yes, I directed the choir of five singers and the 3-piece orchestra. I had never written or arranged a song, never been inside a studio, never played with an orchestra even a rhythm section, and consequently couldn't hold a steady tempo to save my life.

I have to admit that God had given me musical gifts I was not using, but not for lack of desire; more for lack of opportunity. Looking back, it seems clear that God had a plan for my life – a blueprint which, at the time, I couldn't begin to comprehend. I was about to experience another one of those "Five-Minute Windows" that always caught me totally by surprise. But this one would change my life. Forever!

Biggest "Five-Minute Window" of my Life –

During my teaching years, I supplemented my salary with private piano lessons and piano tuning. Minnesota summers were short, so there was always a house or two to be painted. But after my sixth year of teaching, for some reason I couldn't tie down any painting projects. What to do that summer was the question looming in my mind.

It was the last day of my school year. Back in March, a church had requested I tune their piano. "No particular rush" is not the way to make that request. Out of convenience, I postponed the job for three months. Now, at the end of the final school day, I joined my colleagues in the typical round of "Good-byes" and "I'll see you in September," then off to tune a piano that would require much more than the typical 90 minutes.

Having completed the job, I was packing up my kit to leave for home, when a Southern Gospel Quartet came in and started setting up their gear. I knew nothing of this concert. Wow! By just a whisker they missed hearing more honky-tonk sound than Gospel. While I was putting my tools away, one of the singers asked me, "Do you also *play* piano?" I assured him that I did. "Well, could you play a piece for us?" he asked. Most likely I picked out an arrangement I knew well. The singers asked, "Would you mind playing another for us?" They suggested a favorite hymn, and I spun off a quick improvisation.

Their comments were gracious...followed quickly by the question, "Do you happen to have a job?" I had no idea this was an audition. I responded, "Well, it's interesting that you ask. Starting tomorrow, for the first time in my life I *don't* have a job. I'm unemployed for the summer." They quickly informed me that their pianist had resigned that week and they had 90 concerts scheduled in the next 90 days. "If you are interested, could you meet us in Detroit in three days?" I sensed something supernatural transpiring. I said, "This is so sudden. I will need to talk with Diane. But tell me more."

After brief words regarding compensation, they explained that we three men would be alternating two-hour driving shifts (typically through the night). The bus - with three bunk rooms, three tiny sinks, and "minimal" closet space - would be our home for the summer. With some apprehension, I explained that our only son, Scott, was just three months old. This could present some unique space challenges. "No problem" they responded. "We can tack a crib up against the window, and he can enjoy the trip." And enjoy it he did!

As challenging as life in a bus would be, the exhilaration of that summer was unimaginable. We enjoyed experiencing coastal panoramas, Civil War scenes, golfing, deep-sea fishing, travels from Georgia to Maine, and Canadian ventures as far East as Newfoundland. To top it all off, we enjoyed "all-night sings" with the likes of the Blackwoods, Imperials, Couriers, and Cathedrals, rubbing shoulders with - and learning from - the greatest talents in Gospel music.

As I share the rest of this story, don't lose sight of the fact that the "Five-Minute Window" in a Minneapolis church was about as improbable as improbable gets. The piano, most logically, would have been tuned *months* before this concert date. God obviously did have a plan up His sleeve and, even when I didn't see it, He was orchestrating my future behind the scenes. Consider everything that had to happen for Him to complete His orchestration:

- An Atlantic-based quartet, having never sung West of the Mississippi, had to spread their wings beyond the security of the East coast.

- This quartet needed to schedule a concert in Minneapolis at a *date* and *time* which would perfectly coincide with my tuning of a piano.

- For our schedules to match, I would need to postpone for almost 100 days what I'd typically take care of in a week!

- Final "good-byes" to my teaching colleagues would detain my tuning just enough for my path to cross with the quartet's, before finishing the tuning.

- The previous pianist couldn't have delayed giving his resignation by even one week.

- If the piano hadn't been so badly out-of-tune, I would have left the church before the quartet's arrival.

A String of Serendipities –

I've shared with you the fun aspects of a surreal summer adventure which seemed almost like an extended, paid vacation. But let me summarize the musical experiences - compressed into 90 days - that set me on a career path I couldn't have imagined in my wildest dreams.

Song Writing - Until that summer, I had never written a song. My first original composition got its inspiration in the middle of a concert. A second, more inspired song was "God of Miracles," with the lyrics "Speak just a word, and a star will stop in space." When I sang it for the quartet, their response was just the encouragement I needed. They said "That sounds like a Christmas song. Why don't you spin this into a full-blown *musical?*"

Publishing - I hadn't yet been exposed to "The Impossible." Not knowing any better, I barged ahead and that Fall I completed my first of three Christmas musicals. Better yet, *Lillenas* - the first publishing company to hear it - decided to publish and record the musical. Composing original works wouldn't be my life (with a total output of perhaps 50 songs), but the experience was quite rewarding and opened some doors of creative opportunity with industry front-runners like the founder of Brentwood Publishing, Jim Van Hook, who opened some incredible publishing opportunities in the days that followed.

Arranging - Since *songwriting* wasn't my niche, I quickly developed the tools and art of *arranging* existing songs: changing their "feel," altering rhythms, developing counter-melodies, and arranging the pieces for orchestras of various sizes and colors. The most fun was expanding my repertoire of new chords and chord progressions, especially in the Jazz arena. For every original song I wrote, I *arranged* 100 songs. Over the years, the writing for recording, publishing, etc., has exceeded 6,000 arrangements.

Studio Sessions - Since our group, the King's Keynotes, had multiple connections, they received many requests to help budding artists produce recording projects. The Goss Brothers, actually younger than I, formed the rhythm section for numerous projects recorded in the Baldwin Studios of Harrisburg, PA. At that time, no one knew that Larry Goss would become one of the premiere arrangers for the Brooklyn Tabernacle Choir and numerous mainline artists.

Looking back, I'm somewhat embarrassed at my lack of studio qualifications. I still remember a session in which my tempo wasn't totally in control. And I still recall Larry pointing out bar 39 and noting that "the tempo seems to be rushing a bit here. Let's see if we can tighten it up." Since he and his brothers synced with each other like a Swiss clock, it didn't take long to figure out that I was the "Johnny" who was out of step.

First Piano Album - The Keynotes suggested that I produce my first piano project at their expense. The price was right, and this was the first of some 20 personal projects I released over the next 40 years.

Orchestral Arranging - Up until that time, Gospel quartets typically recorded with a *rhythm section* - like the one provided by the Goss Brothers - consisting of *piano, drums, bass, plus a guitar or two.* But suddenly some groups and soloists were developing a taste for more orchestral sounds. The Keynotes decided to follow suit, setting up sessions with a cross section of the Atlanta Symphony. Again, green as a cucumber, I found myself orchestrating the project while bouncing down the highway in our home on wheels. I recall making all the mistakes in the book but concluding, "This is just plain fun. I think I could really enjoy the lifestyle, if I could only figure out how to write an orchestration."

Conducting - One of the most fulfilling and exciting spin-offs of this 90-day experience was meeting an incredible group of guys. The Couriers, consisting of Neil Enloe, Duane Nicholson and Dave Kylonnen, not only were setting a high bar spiritually, but musically reinventing the gospel quartet wheel. Harmonically, they were cranking out fresh, chord progressions – a magical blend of jazz and gospel – unheard of on the gospel circuit. As a pianist, I was *going to school,* literally mesmerized by the voicings in Neil's arrangements. The biggest surprise may have been hearing them pull it off with *just three voices*!

I was completely blown over when *they* asked *me* to arrange their next project for orchestra. Not just any orchestra but specifically *The London Orchestra.* This experience opened the door for many more sessions: in London...as well as in Tel-Aviv, Nashville, and elsewhere.

In Retrospect - Looking back on a lifetime of experiences in music, I find it unimaginable that almost all of them were offshoots of just one summer that might never have happened. The whole domino string pivoted around one <u>narrow</u> "Five-Minute Window" plucked out of one *wide* three-month window in time. No intentionality on my part. *God,* alone, demonstrated his incredible ability to weave together all of the elements of time and space to accomplish, in my world, the plans that only He could conceive.

The Best Was Yet to Come –

After that summer I realized God was taking me on a journey with possibilities I could not have dreamed. Perhaps teaching or performing were not the only career options. With seven years of teaching under my belt, I qualified for a Sabbatical leave. I pursued and completed a Ph.D. in music, not knowing where that pursuit might lead. After ten years of teaching, I simply made myself available, wherever that might take me.

Immediately two college positions surfaced, though that career seemed to have lost its appeal. That same summer, *Bill Gaither* had just completed building an excellent recording studio in Indiana. The Gaither Trio had recently become in great demand, introducing a new genre of songs that were taking the country by storm. Bob MacKenzie filled the role of scouting for studio personnel and a weekend concert pianist. Bob approached me regarding my possible interest in that post. Anyone would concede that such an opportunity would be an enviable position.

The same month, a third option showed up. *Denver First Church of the Nazarene* was emerging as one of the fastest growing churches in the nation. Its *"Saturday Nights In Denver" (S.N.I.D.) concert series* was so successful, it eventually served as the catalyst for many similar concert series across the country. I was offered the position of Arranger for its very innovative television series. Unlike that era's typical TV program featuring lots of "live" preaching, this unique *half hour of 75% music* was professionally studio-recorded. With Denver's incredible proximity to the Rocky Mountains, the video was shot in beautiful locations such as Central City, Estes Park, old gold mining towns, and the Silverton-Durango railroad.

Our thriving church was the dream and brainchild of Pastor Don Wellman. At a time when full-time music positions were as scarce as hen's teeth, Wellman had hired Ken Tippitt as fulltime Choir Director and TV Producer. So it was hard to imagine that a *second* person would be hired, fulltime, as Arranger and Director of Instrumental Music. Not only was Pastor Wellman a visionary leader, but he was secure enough to allow me the freedom of any personal entrepreneurial pursuits, while employed by the church, knowing they would only enhance my ministry with the church.

Three fulfilling offshoots resulted from that 37-year career:

1. With my two boys, Scott and Brad, we built our own *"Eagles Nest" recording studio* on Conifer Mountain in the Rockies. *(See Chapter 5)*
2. We became the originators of Performance Tracks for both the church and school markets. This tool is now used by musicians throughout the world. The result of our efforts was a complete catalog of sing-along Performance Tracks for use by choirs in 108,000 schools and thousands of Christian performers and recording artists. I can't believe we mortgaged our home to buy 216,000 postage stamps. Thankfully we recovered our costs the first year.
3. At the request of *Ralph Carmichael*, one of the great jazz arrangers of the century, I assembled a choir of 1,000 singers to back up his 18-piece Big Band for a concert in

Denver's Mc Nichol's basketball arena. On its heels, many of those singers wanted more opportunities. That's when we gave birth to *the Rocky Mountain Choir and Orchestra*. That aggregation of 400 singers and 60-piece orchestra provided a musical memory and a ministry outlet to musicians for almost 20 years.

The Best Is Still to Come –

Each of us has been on a journey. You and I are *still* on that journey. Thousands of life's events and choices play into the future: where that venture will take us; the cities where we will live; where we attend school; the person we marry – or our children marry; the career path we follow; the promotion we receive or fail to receive. Every occurrence has a domino effect.

The life-changing story which you've just read illustrates how a single, isolated event can totally change every aspect of our lives. For me, it blossomed out of one very slim "five-minute window," while walking out a church door.

As you seek to discover God's roadmap for your life, I would encourage you to do what I and many others are doing. *Journal* the journey, as it opens on a whole world of excitement, serendipity experiences, and providential twists and turns. In the process, you'll find yourself saying, as I have said: "Wow! You just can't make these things up!"

After assembling a 1,000-voice choir for arranger, Ralph Carmichael, the effort blossomed into this 400-voice "Rocky Mountain Praise Choir".

Jerry enjoyed 37 years of ministry at Denver First Church where he developed a 40-piece orchestra. They played every Sunday morning plus special concerts.

A rather unorthodox approach to playing "I'll Fly Away." Jerry loves weaving humorous antics into his concerts. This one always makes for a great ice-breaker.

Seven hands performing all at once?

Why not? The piano has seven octaves!

Quik Stop – C H A P T E R   N I N E

- You've now read just a half dozen stories of strangers linking up with total strangers half way around the world. And there are more incidents – most of them shoe-horned into "Five-Minute Windows." Is this beginning to feel like a hand of Providence may be pulling some strings? If so, it demonstrates the hand of a *relational* God desiring to be an active player in our world.

- Considering all of your jobs or careers, is there one or more which you considered was not your fit?

- If so, were you tempted to think the job was not part of *God's* plan because it didn't seem to "fit?"

- Do you feel that a job which didn't fit you might be simply a job to grow you, mature you, or prepare you for the job down the line that will "fit" perfectly?

- If your present career is that perfect fit, what person(s) or circumstances occurred to open that door?

- What job or jobs have you lost that you thought were a perfect "fit?"

- What sort of job can you think of that might "fit" and be just hanging out around the corner?

Caution:

Recalling that brilliant insight from Chapter One, we have two tendencies: "We *choose* to believe because we *want* to"…or …"We choose to *not* believe because we *don't* want to."

If you sincerely *don't* want to believe that "angels" are visibly active in this world, you might consider skipping this next chapter. You might run a strong risk of changing your mind.

C H A P T E R   T E N

Angels In Disguise

As told by Dr. Jim Diehl

Most of the book you are holding consists of stories from my own journal, entitled "All of His Benefits." You may recognize that title from a verse which reads "Forget not all of His benefits ... [He] who fills your life with good things" (Psalm 103:2-4 *NLT*). Among those good things has been my friendship with *Dr. Jim Diehl*, a colleague who was also my Pastor before becoming a District Superintendent in our church and ultimately elected General Superintendent – the highest office in our denomination world-wide.

Jim is an incredible story-teller. But I asked him to recall a true, specific, hair-raising incident from his own journey. It will give you goosebumps. If you question the existence of angels, you may be about to change your mind. Jim, take it away.

□   □   □   □   □

In August of 1984 I drove from our home in Hastings, Nebraska to Canon City, Colorado to preach in an area-wide camp meeting. The nightly services were held at a rodeo arena with a flatbed truck serving as our platform. After the Friday night's service, two pastor couples came to me asking if I would be open to joining them on a rafting trip Saturday mid-morning on the nearby Arkansas River. Of course, being a flatlander from Iowa and Nebraska, I quickly responded "YES!" I'd always dreamed of that, but there were no raging rivers in Nebraska where I could satisfy the urge.

Before I tell you about the "float trip," let me explain what I DIDN'T know about the situation. I didn't know that Pastor Gene and Nola Haynes had just purchased the rubber raft the week before…or that this was to be its maiden voyage down the river. I didn't know it had been intensely raining in the high country of Colorado for several days and that the Arkansas River was at maximum, springtime, snowmelt level. I didn't know that before such a rafting trip in Colorado, each person needed a helmet, full upper body life vest, and proper shoes. I didn't know that river rapids have names…or that we were about to launch on *the* *"widow maker."* I didn't know that *commercial* rafters use long oars – not short, stubby ones – to maneuver their rafts. I certainly didn't know that an average of 12 to 15 persons drown every year rafting on Colorado rivers.

Gene and Nola Haynes, Dale and Sharon Dieter, and their ten-year-old son, Brian, arrived at my motel room mid-morning on Saturday, August 18th. The six of us headed out to drive upstream from the Royal Gorge on highway 50 to take our historic river raft trip. When we arrived at the secluded spot, we popped the rubber raft off the top of the car; grabbed the two short, stubby oars; put on our horse-collar type vests; and headed for the river. I offered to push the raft into the raging river with the other five in their places on the raft; and I yelled, "This is either going to be the ride of our lives, or we'll all be written up in the Herald of Holiness. [5] We'd most likely show up in the obituary column. Either way, "LET'S GO!"

When I pushed into the current of the river and jumped in, it wasn't thirty seconds before the raft was spinning around in circles. The current was incredible!!! Gene and Nola had the oars; and the last thing I heard was, "ROW, NOLA, ROW! ROW, NOLA, ROW!" In just moments, the raft hit a large boulder in the middle of the river, flipped upside down, and all six of us were hurled into the raging current. The others were evidently thrown out closer to the river's bank, but I was tossed into the middle of the waters where the roaring current started smashing me into one rock after another. The rush of the river was so powerful, I couldn't grab onto anything. In fact, I started rolling head over heels in the spiraling turbulence.

Even though I was a flatlander, I knew I had to hold my breath when I was under water and gasp for air when I surfaced. The highway runs adjacent to the river. Evidently cars were stopping and voices shouting, "People in the river!"

A Lady In Red – As I came up for a moment of air, I saw a lady running down the highway. She was dressed in red slacks and some kind of a red and white shirt. Back under the water I went! Of course my baseball cap was long gone. Then I felt the force of the river tear off both of my tennis shoes. I knew I was bleeding from my chest to my feet after slamming into the gigantic rocks of this violent, swirling, mountain river.

I surfaced again and caught a glimpse of the lady in red…. Running and keeping pace with me beside the river. Down again I went, then up for a gasp of air. The lady in red was still with me! Finally, I was thrown against a huge rock. Only with God's help did I manage to clamp my arms in a death grip around it. I had taken in so much water, I couldn't talk. I managed only to cough and spit.

The lady in red worked her way down the embankment and yelled something to me. All I could do was sputter and spit; so, instantly, she plunged into the raging Arkansas River and came close by. I wrapped my arms around her in another death grip;

and she literally dragged me to the bank of the river, where I sprawled out like a dying fish. By then, men had made their way down the slope to drag me up to the highway's edge.

When they grabbed me, I sputtered and asked, "Where's the lady? Where's the lady in red?" Unbelievably their response was, "We didn't *see* any lady." I assured them I didn't get out of the river by myself. A *lady in red* <u>had</u> pulled me out! Again they insisted, "We didn't see *any* lady."

Finally, sitting on the highway, with a small crowd gathering, I was sputtering, coughing, and trying to answer their questions. "How many in your party?" I responded, "Six". One said, "We have five accounted for. One's missing!" About that time Gene and Nola, Dale and Sharon came down the highway with helpful people assisting them as well. We were all hugging each other – laughing, crying and sputtering; when Sharon cried out, "WHERE'S BRIAN? WHERE'S *BRIAN*?" Oh no! Brian is the one still in the river!

It couldn't have been a minute before a young ten-year-old boy came running down the highway toward us. IT WAS BRIAN!! Such hugs like you've never seen from his Mom and Dad…. And from *all* of us. EVERYBODY WAS HUGGING EVERYBODY!! Brian then remarked, "When the raft capsized, my feet got caught in the rope. Nola unraveled it and shoved me to the bank. Oh Nola, you were a life-saver."

Another Angel? – Nola replied, "Brian, I never saw you. I was thrown clear of the raft and never did see you." Brian responded, "Then *some* lady grabbed me, pulled my feet free, and shoved me toward the bank!"

I couldn't help but wonder, "Might she have been *dressed in red*?"

This awesome miracle unfolded on Saturday, August 18, 1984. I've thought about it a thousand times since then … maybe ten thousand times. I should have drowned. A professional rafting guide who was behind us and witnessed it all said, later: "You were in the river 10 to 12 minutes."

I really should have drowned! But a lady dressed in red rescued me, then just disappeared. I BELIEVE SHE WAS AN ANGEL. If you don't believe that God still has angels (some of whom are dressed in red), it's okay. BUT I WAS THERE.

Lord, when I get to heaven, will you introduce me to that angel? I want to give her a big "THANK YOU" hug.

About a year later, having moved to Colorado, I drove down highway 50 and up that winding road adjacent to the Arkansas River and found the site of that miraculous rescue. I worked my way down to the river and stood there a L-O-N-G time…looking, listening, remembering, and thanking God. Then I saw a stick in the river caught between two big rocks. I made my way down, pulled it out, and again said, "Thank you, Jesus!" That stick is in my office today. It will forever be a symbol of God's grace and mercy during the crisis moment, years before.

I saw. I heard. I was carried. I believe! I KNOW I SAW AN ANGEL!

Later when reflecting on that momentous event in my life, I was reading Psalm 91:11 *KJV*, "For He shall give His angels charge over you, to keep you in all your ways. In their hands they shall bear you up, lest you dash your foot against a stone." God dispatched an angel on August 18, 1984. And I will be forever grateful!

Dr. Jim Diehl

Quik Stop – C H A P T E R   T E N

- On a scale of 1 to 10, how compelling was this story?
- How is the miracle more compelling because it involved two miracle rescues?
- If it was more than twice as believable, what statistical principle (Chapter 4) would come into play?
- What characteristic(s) or behaviors of this particular angel would make the miracle even more convincing?
- If you've had some doubts about the reality of "Heaven," did this story make you more convinced? Why or why not?
- Few people will deny this miracle. The angel was not a 225-pound male athlete. Instead, a slender *woman* walking *alone* on a road at the bottom of the Royal Gorge… doing her assignment, then… disappearing. But *two* rescue miracles of this magnitude is mind-blowing. That grabs my attention.

The large contingency of witnesses on the river bank and inside the rafts, is final added confirmation. And let's not forget where angels come from. Yes, I am personally convinced that "Heaven Is For Real."

Caution:

If you would choose to *not* believe in the possibility of a person going to heaven and returning, because you don't *want* to believe that is possible, you may wish to consider skipping the next chapter.

C H A P T E R   E L E V E N

Out of this World

C olton Burpo was a very typical, quite ordinary lad in most respects. As the years have sped by, he has matured into one of the finest, most humble young men we know. Rachel and I sat across a table in the mountains, totally mesmerized, as he related his astounding story. It will amaze you as it did us.

The Colton Saga –

Colton's father, Todd, was a pastor in the tiny town of Imperial, Nebraska. While Todd was at meetings in Greeley, Colorado, Colton's Mom, Sonja, was at school, teaching. Colton, having complained of a sore stomach, was just three-years, ten-months old and was being cared for by a close friend, Norma. By midday, Sonja received a call that Colton's condition had nose-dived with fever and chills.

The shadow of death – Abdominal pain, profuse vomiting, in and out of fever; the situation sounded like a possible case of appendicitis, a recurring condition in their family. The symptoms were misdiagnosed, eventually ending in a ruptured appendix. The poison had overwhelmed his body for 4 or 5 days and was running unrestrained like a stampeding bull. Colton was quickly driven to the regional hospital in North

Platte, Nebraska. Todd had seen this "shadow of death" many times as a pastor. The skin loses its color. Breathing is labored. Eyes are open, but "nobody's home." Worse yet is the sinking, darkening around the eyes.

Five years earlier, Sonja had been overwhelmed with grief when she'd miscarried two months into the pregnancy. Now it looked for all the world like they could be losing another child. In times like these, it's easy to begin questioning the wisdom of the Almighty. Sonja voiced what seemed inevitable: "Todd, I think this is it."

While surgeons labored intensely to clear up their son's toxic condition, they had all but given up hope. Sonja was on the phone in the lobby begging church members to pray, pray, pray. Todd was alone in another small room, raging at God ... and praying his heart out.

Hope springs eternal – Ninety minutes later a nurse emerged with the news that Colton was out of surgery but screaming relentlessly. How can this be? A minute before, doctor's felt they had done all they could as Colton was teetering over the precipice of death's canyon. To Todd, the screaming was music to his ears; for Colton was begging to see his Dad. A smile crossed his son's face, signaling that the long sting of waiting was over.

Then came words that were a total surprise: "Daddy, you know I almost died." Todd perked up immediately. Was his boy repeating something the lad had overheard the medical staff say? This was impossible, since he'd been under sedation the entire time! A whole constellation of miracles was about to follow. Imagine their surprise to learn that, during surgery, *Colton was aware* of his father in a small room crying his heart out at God while, at the same time, his mother was in another room on her cell phone begging for prayers. Todd was absolutely floored. How could this be possible under sedation?

The rest of Colton's story remained a mystery for four months. Only then did Colton's parents become even more convinced that something strange had happened. Little by little, fragments of his conversations suggested that, during surgery, he had had an encounter that only begged more questions!

A volley of miracles unfolds – With rapid fire speed, insights like these begin to emerge from Colton's lips: "Dad, I was sitting on Jesus' lap."[6] "Did you know Jesus has a cousin? His cousin baptized Him." Colton then described how Jesus' clothes were white, but Jesus was the only One in heaven with a purple sash (illustrating how it ran across Jesus' chest).

Weeks later, while riding down the highway with his Father, Colton spoke up: "Dad, you had a Grandpa named 'Pop,' didn't you? I got to stay with him."[7] Todd had never spoken one word of Colton's *Great*-Grandfather. Grandfathers, yes, but not *Great*-Grandfathers. In fact, Pop had died 34 years before Colton was born and would be 89 years older!

Two sisters? – What ultimately got Sonja's attention was when her son remarked that he had *two* sisters. The comment stopped her in her tracks like nothing ever had. "But Colton, do you mean your sister and cousin, Traci?" Colton was suddenly adamant. "No, mommy. I have two *sisters*. You had a baby die in your tummy, didn't you?" A miscarriage had never been discussed with any of the children! Colton continued, "In Heaven, she ran up to me and wouldn't stop hugging me." Ironically, it took a little four-year-old boy to inform his parents that the child they lost was, in fact, a girl; and someday they would see her in Heaven.[8]

As time went on, Colton revealed that he was in the throne room of God. "Well, Colton, where was God?" Todd asked. "He was in this big chair." (Colton had no idea what a 'throne' was.) "And where was Jesus?" "He was sitting on a chair right here." Colton pointed to the chair on the right side of God. "Well, who sits on the other side of God's chair?" Todd asked. Confidently Colton responded, "That's where the angel Gabriel is. He's really nice."

As the months flew by, more and more insights spilled from young Colton's memory. Each time Todd or Sonja saw a painting or sketch of Jesus, they would ask Colton, "Is this like Jesus?" or "What's wrong with this one?" Without hesitation he would respond, "No, it's just not Him." One evening, Todd was glancing through some website photos and came across a painting entitled "Prince of Peace." Showing it to Colton, the boy gazed into the eyes of Jesus for a moment, then responded with no hesitance, "DAD, THIS ONE'S RIGHT!"[9]

Sequel to the Colton Saga –

Colton's response is not at all surprising when you know the unbelievable origin of the "Prince of Peace" painting. Akiane (Ah-kee-ah-na) was the name given the painter as a tiny infant. Since her parents were self-proclaimed atheists, there was no Bible. No church. Essentially zero outside religious influence. "The concept of God never was discussed in their home. But God quickly became a part of [Akiane's] daily life … as visions of God [Jesus] started when she was just four."[10]

Akiane's unique story is better told in her own book and in her words on a YouTube Video[11] where she describes her *disappearance* at the age of five. It was during this time she gathered impressions of Heaven which began to show up in subsequent paintings. The You Tube video illustrates, in super-fast motion, her stroke-by-stroke painting of a portrait of Jesus.

At the remarkable *age of eight,* she painted *Jesus, Prince of Peace* – her most treasured work and one which is now recognized around the world.   If you will Google "Painting The Impossible," the unimaginable detail to her painting will blow your mind. This video is well worth 25 minutes of your time!

By now you have discovered an almost inconceivable miracle. What are the odds that Colton would, with no hesitation, pick Akiane's painting out of scores of images of Jesus?   It's no surprise at all. The irony is that both he and Akiane had the rare experience of seeing Jesus, the Prince of Peace, *in Person*!

The rest of the story is pretty much history. It was a full seven years after the Heaven journey when Colton was eleven years old, that the book *Heaven is for Real* was released topping the New York Times best seller list for weeks. The subsequent movie, also featured Akiane's *Prince of Peace* painting, which, likewise, quickly became a phenomenon across the globe. The *Heaven Is for Real* movie, book and translations in 24 languages have, together, shared the hope of Heaven with an estimated 35 to 40 million people.

My Personal Reflections –

I must tell you, I have never given any serious thought to the possibility of a person being swept up into Heaven. Then I recalled the Apostle Paul's story of an experience like the one you've just reviewed. It was so astounding and "inexpressible" that, unfortunately, he wasn't allowed to talk about it. And I recall the Apostle John, writer of the book of Revelation, being swept up into heaven in the same fashion (by an angel) and, thankfully, documenting everything he saw and heard. But John's experience was destined to be the go-to source for all we would *need* to know about this Celestial destination. In Chapter 16 we'll take a very close-up look at John's Heaven experience as he details everything he saw and heard.

As I thought about Colton's unusual encounter, I realize there are some who would deny that this event even happened. If so, how would they explain the unbelievable volley of miracles that followed? How could he have known his Mom was on the phone, begging for prayers, while his Father was praying in another room? And what of the Great-Grandfather who met him, of all places, in the Throne Room of God? And the sister who embraced and welcomed him by name! A sister he never knew he had! A sister that his parents didn't even know *was* a "sister."

These are just a few among a long string of miracles springing from Colton's memory. I must either deny an experience that I'm convinced God Himself had orchestrated … or attribute it to some Satanic counterfeit. I would think Heaven is the last destination Satan would choose to offer *anyone*.

Sequel to the Sequel –

This chapter in my personal story is a sequel to Akiane's story … which was the logical sequel to Colton's story.

One day I was perusing one of the many YouTube listings for which *Time* magazine has become recognized. I chanced upon a list of the "One hundred most influential persons in all of history."[12] Most of them made the world a better place. Others gained their notoriety and influence because of their extensive *negative* impact on the world at large. *Jesus* obviously had to make the list. *Who else* in history has blessed the lives of more people? Who else has established a following of more than two billion people? What other leader has died and lived to tell about it?

As I was introducing my new arrangement of the "Hallelujah Chorus," in the process I was showing images of ten of these most influential persons. When it came to finding an image of Jesus, however, I was faced with a dilemma. Combing through several websites, each one featured from 150 to 300 different Jesus portraits.

Having never seen Jesus in person as Colton and Akiane had (and, at that point in time, had never heard of either person), my focus was simply on finding a portrait that I *thought* might come close to Jesus' features. Finding nothing on the first website, I moved on to the next. The more images I scanned, the faster I flipped through more than 200 thumbnail photos and sketches of Jesus: smiling, laughing, serious, seated, standing, and even knocking at a door. Finally, my eyes fell on a portrait entitled "Prince of Peace." I was so overwhelmed that I came to a screeching halt. This "coincidental," serendipity experience I realized months later, shouldn't have surprised me at all.

Just as God led Colton to discover Akiane's incredible, inspired painting, after three years of nodding and saying "No, that's not the one," it's hard to imagine that my against-the-odds discovery of the *very same image* could have been by happenstance or pure luck. Quite the opposite. With odds of 1 in 300 or so, it was like *God Himself* was flipping through the hundreds of likenesses. I didn't need an excursion beyond this universe to see Jesus in Person. This portrait made me feel like, as one song suggests, "I've Just Seen Jesus!"

Quik Stop – C H A P T E R   E L E V E N

- Without glancing back, identify as many miracles as you can recall springing from this story. These would take the form of revelations or discoveries by Colton or his parents which would not likely have been possible without some miraculous intervention.

- On a scale of 1 to 10, how compelling is this story and the string of miracles?

- How does the *Akiane* sequel make this chapter even more believable – or not?

- What about the sequel to the sequel makes the story even more compelling – or not?

- Could these "coincidences" be considered examples of "exponential" improbability? (see Chapter 4)

- What reasons might God have had to single out such a young person (3 years, 10 months) for a brief journey to Heaven?

- Are you more inclined to believe in Heaven or are you unchanged having read this chapter? (Regarding the first question, there were 8 or 9 miracles or discoveries cited in this chapter).

C H A P T E R   T W E L V E

Devil's Advocate

I f you and I come from very different directions in our beliefs, let me salute you for staying with this book. The stories may have been rather casual reading. However, I think the upcoming chapters will present even more exciting challenges.

If you ever took a high school or college course "Debate 101," you've played the role of "Devil's Advocate" (D.A.) – challenging an opinion or position which you may not, yourself, believe or embrace.

Let me ask how you may have explained away some of these stories:

- My fuel pump story with the Angel in the Fargo salvage yard (Chapter 2) – Or the "Angel in the Jungle" (Chapter 7) – Or "Ambush at Galilee" (Chapter 3) where an unseen hand rerouted us around an ambush that might have terminated our lives. A seasoned debater may have explained away some of the details in these stories.

- But how might you have scrambled to explain away Jim Diehl's angelic rescue while drowning in the spiraling, turbulent "Widowmaker?" (Chapter 10). Jim saw the lady in red. The tourists did not. Why? Because angels don't hang out for autographs, front page stories and photo ops. They simply…disappear. Finding a plausible explanation for TWO simultaneous angel-rescues, unseen by tourists at the very scene, presents a much steeper challenge for any debater. We call that an "exponential improbability."

• The plot thickens when you get to Colton's story (Chapter 11) and struggle to explain where he went during an hour-and-a-half, death-grip, lights-out surgery. "In body" or "out of body" – call it what you wish. But how does one explain his awareness of both his Mom's and Dad's location while under sedation and dangling over the canyon of death? The volley of hospital witnesses only complicates a major debating challenge, not to mention the huge constellation of miracles.

• All of the above are rudimentary challenges for a D.A. compared to the story you'll read in later chapters.

Contemporary D.A.s –

I recently viewed a preacher on You-Tube who adamantly squelched *any and all* Heaven-and-back stories. Glossing over Apostle John's heaven-encounter and Apostle Paul's glowing approval of a similar encounter, he posed a question; in effect: "if these stories are true, why weren't there dozens more heaven-visitor stories from back then?"

My first thought, in response was "How can you say there were *not* such stories?" Consider the challenges:

1. Not being written by *Apostles*, their books wouldn't likely make the cut when the New Testament was assembled.

2. Preserving books for 2,000 years using papyrus and scrolls, was a process reserved mainly for recognized philosophers and authors of Biblical writings.
3. Lacking any method of duplication or distribution, why not just *tell* the stories? In fact, that's most likely what they did. We'll simply never be blessed by *their* stories.

Another common assumption: Most of us have heard statements such as "There won't be pets in heaven; Jesus never spoke a word about it." Let's take a look at this absurd surmise.

Very little of Jesus' speaking was recorded. The four Gospel writers, Matthew, Mark, Luke and John captured only 1% to 2% of the words Jesus spoke in His last three years! The Scriptures tell us that many of Jesus' miracles were not recorded. And if all of them were, "I suppose that even the world itself would not contain the books which were written" (John 21:25 *NASB*). Recall this fact next time you hear someone say "Jesus never spoke a word about it."

Biblical D.A.s –

Devil's Advocates are sprinkled throughout the Bible. The scuttlebutt on the street following Jesus' Resurrection, was that His disciples must have stolen His body and run off with it (Matthew 28:11-15). They had no plausible explanation for getting past the 24-hour military watch. They only knew *He couldn't possibly be alive.*

The account of Jesus restoring 20-20 vision to a blind man is totally fascinating (John 9:1-34). Jesus came up with this home-spun, pharmaceutical concoction consisting of "spit and mud"; and the man's eyes were instantly healed, as soon as Christ touched them. Suddenly the most hardened D.A.s (the Pharisees) came out of the woodwork. They knew the sighted one well as a blind man; and now they saw him walking without a cane. Their bias totally stymied any sensible response.

With blind impulsiveness, the Pharisee D.A.s would come up with a charge, against Christ, that was totally off the wall. Ignoring the miracle before their eyes, they invented the ridiculous accusation that Jesus was healing on the Sabbath – an act which made Him a sinner. What did this have to do with the miracle? They probed the blind man for an explanation. I love his response: "I know nothing about that (their accusation) … But I know one thing for sure: I was blind…I now see" (John 9:25 *MSG*). How can you argue with *that?*

To Heaven and Back – Believe It or Not –

You may have been thinking that this Heaven-and-back phenomenon is something new and unprecedented. Reading Apostle John's account in the book of Revelation, I get the impression that he was "*in* the body" while being hosted throughout the city by an angel.

On the other hand, I cited one person who would deny the idea of any "*out* of body" experience such as Colton confirmed, insisting that such a thing is impossible.

Apostle Paul's position – There is valuable insight to gain from the Apostle Paul whose friend was, in Paul's words, "caught up into the 3rd Heaven (thought to be the uppermost Throne Room of God). Most scholars believe that Paul, himself, was that person but didn't want to draw attention to the special revelation God was giving him. If the person *was* Paul himself, it makes "Heaven and back" stories all the more plausible.

There are two observations worth pointing out: *First* of all, Paul cared not whether this experience was "in the body" or "out of body." In fact, Paul admits to not even knowing in which state the visit took place. *Secondly*, his enthusiasm for what this man experienced was evident in his comment, "[This man] whether in the body or out of the body I do not know, only God knows, was caught up into Paradise ... on behalf of such a man and his experiences *I will boast"* (II Cor. 12:2 *AMP*).

Fabricated stories? – In the previous chapter, I inferred that there may be some perils to buying into just *any* "free pass to Heaven" story that happens along. I Peter 2 speaks of frauds who, in the last days, will introduce destructive heresies and false teachings.

In contrast to Colton's very credible story, a different young boy recuperating from a tragic car accident, fabricated a journey to Heaven. With his father, they published a book and sold a very huge number of copies. Later on, overcome with guilt, the boy confessed his wrongdoing. I admire his courage; His confession was honest and very sincere though his efforts to rectify his sin by removing all book references from social media and distribution sources have met with dead-ends.

Most of us have heard of "healers" who have actually colluded with someone to simulate what is really a 'fake' healing. But if you believe in miraculous restoration to health, you don't cease to pray for someone's healing ... just because you heard about a scammer. Throw out the bath water – but save the baby!

Why Sample Just Colton Burpo? – Four reasons:

1. I started into this book with five very reputable "Heaven-visitors." But our focus isn't so much *about* Heaven as *how you can be sure* you are going there.
2. Colton passed my "six steps" (see next page) with flying colors.
3. Besides Colton's credibility, his experiences teach us many things about Heaven which are not only consistent with God's word, but also incredibly validated when compared

with the conclusions of authority, Dr. Alcorn. (Refer to pgs. 113 – 114 in this book.)

4. Perhaps most important, I looked for someone who had read NOTHING about heaven (or the Bible), had no ulterior motives, possessed childlike innocence and was unaffected with being sort of "hand-picked" by God. What better fit could one find than a naïve, 3-year, 10-month-old tot?

This Writer's Position – Let me assure you that, like Paul, my focus is not to promote "free-pass-to-Heaven" stories. For that reason my concert ministry intentionally avoids promoting those stories. I choose to focus, instead, on helping people discover the joys of knowing, personally, the One Who has gone to prepare a place for those who have embraced His gift of eternal life.

SIX TESTS: For Real or Not For Real? – Millions of people have seen "visions" and have all the marks of credibility. But visions are primarily to edify the person *experiencing* the vision. This discussion is more about persons whom *God* has singled out and who eagerly return to *share* what they witnessed.

To be fair to those who may be skeptical, I feel there are many who believe in *Heaven* but are dubious about the credibility of "Heaven-visitors" simply because they know of one or two whose fabricated stories have proven to be fraudulent.

For that reason, I've adopted *six rigorous tests* which, I believe, offer a very reliable measure of the credibility of a person who claims to have been to Heaven and back.

Using *Colton Burpo* (*Heaven is for Real*) as a model for my observations, consider the below italicized insights:

#1: Scriptural Teaching – Is there anything in his/her story that contradicts the Bible?

It is rather incredible that the accounts of a lad of 3 years and 10 months could be so consistent with Biblical teaching: Jesus' baptism by his cousin; Colton's experiences in the Throne Room – his noting Jesus' position in the right hand "chair". Colton's discovery that Gabriel occupies the "chair" to God's left. None of this *contradicts* the Bible. These details are simply part of a real experience recalled by a 4-year-old. Colton explained to me that he didn't need to defend himself. When people ask questions, he simply tells them "this is what I saw." What else would one *want* to hear from a four-year-old? I believe it's the very reason God *chose* such a young child!

#2: Are there any confirming "miracles" that became part of the person's story?

In Colton's account, there are numerous encounters with the Supernatural, most of which were confirmed over the *months* following his return.

#3: Were there live witnesses to corroborate the person's departure and return?

In Colton's case, there were dozens: His family, church members, doctors, nurses, relatives, his baby sitter and school friends.

#4: Does he/she have anything to gain by immediately telling or selling his/her story?

Colton was not quite 4 years old. Colton's father wrote the documentary book which sold extremely well. But Todd didn't author it for seven years, and he did so only after much persuasion. Financial profit was obviously not on his radar screen.

#5:   *Is there unquestioned documentation of the person's physical state (or, possibly death) at the time of his/her visit to Heaven?*

Colton experienced a near death experience. He was monitored constantly for an hour-and-a-half. Doctors had done all they could to sustain his life. He dangled on the precipice of death by a thread. His soul separated from his body until reunited upon return to earth. The Apostle Paul referred to this as an "Out-of-body," OBE, experience.

#6   **What do I sense in the Heaven-visitor's ongoing ministry that is leading listeners to discover the Person of Jesus Christ?**

Colton and his father, Todd, spent several years sharing their story in churches and on radio and TV. Remarkably, an estimated 35 to 40 million people were touched by their ministry through a documented *movie, DVDs* and by way of books translated into 24 languages. Clearly, God's stamp of approval shined on what I believe was, obviously, God's own idea. For millions, it was their first introduction to the hope of Heaven. (Today the Burpos continue in very active leadership roles in their local churches).

Admittedly, developing a relationship with Colton and his family paved the way for Rachel and me to gain a more close-up, microscopic view of their lives, their commitment to God and their unwavering passion to share the treasured promise of Heaven.

What is the benefit of people visiting Heaven? –

Billy Graham cited a Gallup survey which revealed, sadly, that only 26 percent of Baptists, 20 percent of Lutherans, and 16 percent of Methodists thought their chances of attaining heaven were excellent."[13]

If God's plan is to use these Colton-like experiences to open a wider window for discovering the reality and hope of Heaven, I am liking His plan. In a day of declining faith and morality across the board, we need more people who will passionately share their witness and the hope of Heaven.

Increasing Enthusiasm About Heaven – Foremost Heaven scholar, Randy Alcorn, refers to many people, including *pastors*, who have related their impressions that, in Heaven, spirits soar around in some ethereal, cosmic, foggy ionosphere, singing in a non-stop angelic choir. They speak of such thoughts making them literally depressed.[14] Such a place has no appeal.

If even pastors, with access to the most descriptive commentaries, enter the pulpit with this erroneous impression, why not benefit from the glowing perspectives of Heaven-visitors who are eye-witnesses to a place that so transcends anything we've experienced on this planet. Could it be that this form of revelation has benefits we've never considered?

Billy Graham also pointed out another benefit of near-death-experiences. He noted that "without exception, these life-after-death experiences seem to reduce the fear of dying." [15]

Accounts which I have read speak of a Paradise featuring hills and mountains, lakes and streams and grass emanating light from within – grass manicured to such perfection that the Pebble Beach golf course appears to need a new maintenance crew. What is so astonishing and confirming to me is the consistency of their accounts, but with varying descriptions that personalize each person's impressions.

Richard Sigmund had the most vivid recall, describing children in footraces exceeding the speed of horses … or climbing trees 200 feet high and floating gently down. Many were enjoying games that defy our laws of gravity. Lounging in the bottom of a crystal-pure lake was obviously no threat to their survival.[16]

Those who have been blessed to visit Heaven report on a place that is far more "real" than this ball of mud we now call "home." Sharing their perspective confirms that Heaven is the most "surreal" and genuine of all experiences.

Millions more learning of the "Hope" of Heaven – Colton, Akiane, Don Piper, Mary Neal, Richard Sigmund, Dale Black, Betty Malz and scores of others have shared not only the "reality" of this destination, but the "hope" of Heaven with, collectively, over 100 million people. Millions of those who, otherwise, would never have heard about the hope of Heaven, have discovered a personal relationship with the God of creation. This, being the greatest benefit, was undoubtedly in the mind of God when He selected specific people for a journey to the 'Son.'

Affirming Biblical Accounts – Billy Graham and others have pointed out that much detail about heaven is either not covered in the Bible or is simply inferred. All that we MUST know is found in the book of Revelation and other books by the Apostle John. But that leaves a wealth of curious questions.

Randy Alcorn – the "Go To" source – Dr. Randy Alcorn, authority and author of over 50 books, has written the book "Heaven," which is recognized by most preachers and teachers, as *the* source for such knowledge. With a fine-tooth comb, he has crisscrossed the Bible to provide answers to the most asked questions. Whenever his conclusions might have been speculative, he has made that clear.

What is so astonishing is that, almost 100% of the time, his conclusions have been affirmed by Colton's heaven-accounts. (Incidentally, he had never heard of Dr. Alcorn). Colton's "eyewitness" affirmations, below, make both his and Dr. Alcorn's accounts all the more credible. You might open both books for comparison (see footnotes for book titles). Comments and page numbers are referenced below. Dr. Alcorn's comments are followed by Colton's in *italics*.

- Heaven, and its residents are "physical," not "spirits" –52.
  Colton sat on Jesus' lap in the right hand 'chair' – 63, 98.

- Our identities will not change. We'll even recognize loved ones we've never met – 286, 346.
  Colton recognized, and stayed with, his GREAT-Grand-dad whom he'd never met, and who died and went to heaven 34 years before Colton was born! – 86.

- Contrary to 'politically correctness' we'll retain our gender identity – 295.
  Colton's "sister" introduced herself on his arrival in heaven – 93-97.

- 'Scripture speaks repeatedly about eating in heaven." – 291, 301.
  Colton had mac-and-cheese and all the pizza he wanted – (quoted from a lunch-conversation with Colton, Oct 22, 2020).

- "Apparent" age of the most elderly in heaven was early 30s when they were at their prime in physical characteristics – 297
  Colton didn't recognize pictures of "Pop," (the Great-Grand-Dad he never met) until seeing the photo taken when "Pop" was age twenty-nine – 121.

- Young children continue growing in heaven – 298. *Colton's miscarried sister (age 6, in heaven) was taller than Colton – 95.*

- We will meet and recognize Characters from the Bible – 346.
Colton met Samson, John the Baptist, Angel Gabriel – 99, 64, 101. Also King David, Peter and Mary – quote from Colton lunch meeting, Oct 22, 2020.

- We'll gain in knowledge; Jesus said "learn from me" –318.
Colton's favorite thing about heaven was homework. And why not? He told us that Jesus was his teacher – 71.

- There are angels in heaven – 283.
Colton spoke of angels with wings and 'lights' (halos) on their heads – 72.

- Some people, including martyrs, have a window to view what is happening on earth (Revelation 6:10) – 66. *While in heaven, Colton began to pray for his dad when he saw him weeping and praying his heart out in a small hospital room – 102.*

- Angels, appearing on earth, may assume human form – 52.
Jim Diehl's rescue on the turbulent Arkansas river, was by a lady dressed in red whom observers did not see. (Chapter 10).

Colton at Age 4

Kicking back with Colton – Age 21

Heaven: What We *Must* Know...and What We Don't *Need* to Know –

To be totally clear, everything we absolutely *need* to know about Heaven is revealed in God's Word. However, there will be thousands in Heaven who embraced the Gospel but, lacking any written Scriptures, never knew there was such a place. Relax. Nowhere is it suggested that you have to *know* about Heaven to *get* there. It might simply be an unexpected bonus.

When Jesus promised He was preparing a place for us, He added "I'll come back and get you so you can live where I live." (John 14:4 *MSG*) Now, that's a *"must* know!"

When John wrote that "nothing unclean will ever enter ... only those whose names are written in the Lamb's book of life," he was sharing a *"must* know." But *a wall 216 feet thick and made of jasper* I'd consider "<u>nice</u> to know" or "don't <u>need</u> to know."

When Colton discovered that the left "chair" in the throne room was occupied by the Angel Gabriel, I found that "nice to know," (especially if, someday, the question shows up in a trivia game). Many other "visitors" described flowers you can pick but which don't die when replaced. Also in the "nice to know" category; it makes me all the more excited to get there!

But there are two things I've learned that God has allowed to be shared by those whom He blessed with a brief visit. Granted they are not a *need* to know. However, I would put both in the *"really* nice to know" category.

Will our new bodies be recognized? – One paraphrase, describing these 'tents' we live in, suggests this life on Earth is "like a stopover in an unfurnished shack" (II Cor 5:5, *MSG*). However, we've been promised **brand new** bodies. Children, especially, are fearful that they may not find their Grandparents or Parents. But it isn't just children expressing the concern.

Having lost her husband, an older lady – with trembling voice, posed this question to Billy Graham. He acknowledged that the Bible doesn't answer all of our Heaven questions, but He indicated we will know each other more fully than we do now.

Jesus didn't say he would *change* or *replace* all things; He said He would make all things NEW. We may not *need* to know what this means concerning our new bodies. However, reading at least a half dozen different accounts by Heaven-visitors who have addressed the "apparent age" issue, I find that <u>all</u> of them described acquaintances of 70, 80 and 90 years of age to appear in their "late-20s" or "mid-30s" but retaining all of their original ID traits. *Very* fascinating. All signs of age, wrinkles, lost hair, arthritic hands … are GONE. Yes, in heaven "we will know even as we are known" (I Cor. 13:12 *NIV*).

I can hardly wait to see my new parents. Dad with all his hair and teeth. Mom no longer stooped over from the effects of polio. No glasses. Wrinkles vanished. Crippled fingers now ready for the piano (which she couldn't play down here). But I will recognize them both!

Reading accounts which describe, in some detail, what our new bodies will be like, fits in the "<u>really</u> nice to know" category.

Will miscarried babies be in Heaven? – This would also be "*real* nice to know." It's an honest but perplexing question for many parents who have experienced a miscarriage or who wrestle with the guilt of unnecessary abortions. Yes, it's inferred in the Bible. But I am among those many parents who never translated that inference into reality. The next chapter clearly answers this question.

Quik Stop – C H A P T E R   T W E L V E

- Are you wrestling with the reality of a "Heaven?"
  If so, how does this chapter with Colton's portrayal
  and Apostle Paul's comments, help or not help you to
  accept that Heaven and "Heaven-visitors" are very
  credible and real?

- How many of the *six tests* for reliability of persons
  claiming to have gone to Heaven can you recall?

- What did you learn from this chapter that would be
  considered "not essential" to your salvation or spiritual
  development? Which of these do you consider <u>nice to
  know</u> even though not essential to arriving on
  Heaven's shore?

- How were you affected by the striking comparison
  between Dr. Alcorn's research and Colton Burpo's
  experiences?

- Might a person make it to Heaven even if they didn't
  know there was such a place?

C H A P T E R   T H I R T E E N

When Does Life Really Begin?

Several theories have been floated in an attempt to answer this monumental question. Examining the feedback from those who have visited heaven might give us some clues to help answer this question once and for all.

At the most conservative extreme is what we've come to recognize as the "Pro Life" position, holding to the belief that life begins with that first fertile moment of conception. At the other extreme are those who maintain that life begins at the moment of actual *birth*.

Reconciling the two stances may never be possible. But …

Unwrapping the Mystery –

At this point, you may wish to revisit the part of Colton's story in Chapter 11 where he informs his mother that he met a sister, in Heaven, that greeted him by name and with open arms. It was that sister who, ironically, informed Colton that she had died "in her mommy's tummy" as Colton described it.

Not only had the parents never shared about a miscarriage at two months, but they had no idea the unborn child was a *girl* until Colton, in casual conversation, mentioned her gender to his parents![17]

Here's the long and short of it. If, in God's mind, Colton's sister couldn't even *exist* as a "person" until the moment of birth, she obviously wouldn't be in heaven today. Clearly the decisive "beginning of life" moment had to precede the miscarriage by *two months*! It could only be *the moment of conception*. Where else could one draw the line in the sand? How much more transparent could God have made it? How clever of Him to use a young child to help unwrap this timeless mystery!

A Personal Serendipity – When I read this part of Colton's story for the first time, the phenomenal, life-origin insight powerfully struck home. You see, Diane and I had experienced the grief of a miscarriage over 50 years ago between the births of our sons, Scott and Brad.

Like thousands of parents who have read Colton's story and seen it portrayed in movie and DVD, I recently experienced, *for the first time,* the unimaginable joy that someday I will meet our only daughter in Heaven. I am speaking in "first-person, singular" since that daughter and Diane are already reunited! In September, 2001, Diane stepped on Heaven's shore just hours before the 9-11 attack on New York's twin towers.

Without question, the mystery of life's origin is *inferred* in the Bible itself. But most people, I've discovered, haven't translated that inference into a grand homecoming rendezvous with a child they never met.

There are thousands, like Diane and me, who never discussed someday meeting a child. We moved on with life, eventually losing sight of – or never ever realizing – the huge serendipity experience awaiting us. But, it was Colton's revelation in Heaven that reminded me of the Biblical truth that "*Life begins at Conception,*" not birth. (Psalm 139:15-16, Isaiah 49:5,

Jeremiah 1:5.) And that awesome discovery impacts every victim of abortion as well.

In God's eyes, every child of His creation is precious, valued and *eternal*.

Your DNA Blueprint –

Advocates of the Pro Life position maintain that each life, from its conception, is a unique creation of God and that all of the newborn's DNA components are in place from that very moment. In fact, in some sense, before any child was a glimmer in his or her mother's eyes, they believe that God had already assembled the DNA blueprint.

Not only the *physical* DNA blueprint but also the *soul* and *spirit*! Together these three components comprise the total person, including: our unique personalities, talents; our capacity to remember, think and reason; and even the capacity to feel emotions and express love.

Psalm 139 describes a God who secretly and intricately weaved together the details of my "unformed substance" (Psalm 139:16 *AMP*). In fact, my days were written in His book "when none of them as yet existed" (Psalm 139:16 *NRSV*).

This implies that the gifts and talents He envisioned for me – before I was born – would give shape to my musical tastes, my propensities, the length and strength of my fingers, my personality – all of the characteristics that would ultimately give shape to the future and career He designed for me.

The same intricate plan applies to *you* as well. You were not an "accident." Consider God's words, as shared by Jeremiah: "I know the plans I have for you … plans to give you hope and a future" (Jeremiah 29:11 *NIV*).

If you started into this book assuming the role of a Devil's Advocate, you may be tempted to discount the whole Colton Burpo story; for it shines a blinding light on the "genesis of life" debate.

But, as a D.A., could you shed that hat for just a moment?

As I've suggested, Colton's string of miracles is virtually undeniable. What is so fascinating to me is that God chose a little tike, not yet four years old, to add documented confirmation to the true beginning of a human life. We would be less inclined to trust an adult (someone who knew too much about the "Right to Life" debate, miscarriages, publishing contracts, abortion and all the theological overtones).

God wanted someone illiterate (obviously, by virtue of age), unsophisticated, innocent, totally without pretense. In fact, a child with zero awareness that his providential encounter in Heaven was, in fact, about to open a broader window of perspective surrounding the greatest mystery in the universe; the genesis of life itself!

Quick Stop – C H A P T E R   T H I R T E E N

- What miracle of Colton's helped unravel the mystery of life's origin?
- What three parts of every person's total makeup are a part of their DNA blueprint?
- According to God's scheme in Psalm 139, when do these three components come together?   1) before conception, 2) at time of conception, 3) at birth
- Why do you think God chose such a young child, instead of an adult to return from Heaven with many discoveries and insights?
- Will aborted babies be in Heaven?

CHAPTER FOURTEEN

Beliefs Weren't Born in a Vacuum

One crisp December evening, I stepped onto my patio to retrieve an armful of logs for my fireplace. Arrested by what sounded like a thousand miniature sanding blocks in motion, I flipped on the patio light. Abruptly, the sounds ceased. I flipped off the light. Waiting in silence for a minute, the mysterious sounds resumed, as if on command by an invisible general. I repeated this cycle two or three times.

Finally, kneeling down, I peered between the logs only to discover hundreds of one-inch tall pyramids artfully gracing the tops of the logs. With my pencil I brushed across one of the miniatures. A pile of sawdust grains slid to the floor.

It seems hundreds of pine beetles had teamed up with an insidious plan to destroy my wood pile by nibbling away, one bite at a time, the fibres that would provide warmth and security for the winter.

Similar, I thought, to my neatly stacked core of doctrines providing the secure foundation for all I believe. The culture in which we live is propped up by assumptions that insidiously nibble away at our most fundamental beliefs. One of the most damning, yet popular misconceptions ever contrived: "It doesn't matter what you believe as long as you believe something."

Without sufficient evidence, you may *choose* to believe the world is flat. Wrong as it turned out to be, we must at least admit that, in the grand scheme of things, the error was of virtually no serious consequence. No one was reported as falling off the edge in quest of Hawaii.

But one misguided assumption was of most incalculable consequence when one Adolf Hitler, sincerely *believing* that "the end (by his standards) justifies the means," wiped millions of unsuspecting victims from the planet. The same erroneous belief took down the towers on 9-11.

Heaven Visitors and Angels –

Issues such as these have generated more debate, opinion and conflicting bias than most any other peripheral doctrine. What is so surprising is that the Apostle Paul is so clear on the "Heaven-and-back" subject. Some of us, one day, may find ourselves in a circle enjoying some chuckles over revelations on issues where we spent so much time spinning our wheels.

This Writer's Position – How do I, personally, handle the subject in my piano concerts? I don't. It's that simple. I'll share the hope of Heaven and what I know about that awesome destination, but my focus is this: "How can I point my audience toward discovering the *hope* of heaven?"

I have discussed (not debated) this subject with a number of people. I don't recall any of them ever referring to a book they have read by someone claiming to have made the trip to Heaven. Debating some sensitive subjects, I believe, runs the risk of driving a wedge, unnecessarily, in a relationship where the issue is not of any eternal consequence.

This may well be one of those subjects where most people will *not* believe because they simply don't *want* to.

What Beliefs Are Worth Dying For? Perhaps a more salient question is this: "What determines if a belief is worth bleeding or dying for?" I have a simple answer to that question. If it has any bearing on one's *eternal destiny*, it is worth dying for. A martyr could likely answer the question without blinking.

Like the Apostle Paul, I commend those who have enjoyed their Heaven experience. In fact, I'd encourage them to share their story. And why? Why else would God have sent them on such an exquisite adventure if not to *share* their story?

The same could be said of the discussions surrounding the subject of angels. My advice? Read Jim Diehl's story in Chapter 10 before you decide *not* to believe in angels.

A friend of mine once offered a nugget of wisdom in easy-to-understand language when he said: "Don't get all wrapped around the axle over matters you can't understand nor explain and often can't defend. There are bigger fish to fry."

Why Do We Believe What We Believe? –

As we tackle this monumental question, let's keep in focus that intuitive insight from Chapter One. It's worth restating: "Not realizing the hazards, we tend to believe [whatever it is we believe because] we *want* to believe." Conversely "We *don't* believe because we simply don't *want* to believe."

I have suggested that simply *wanting* to be a Christian or an Atheist or a Buddist is not a good enough reason. I am what I am as the result of a personal search. It is a *choice* but one which I *own* based on reasons I can fully embrace. Good, bad or indifferent, what are some reasons that we believe what we believe?

Peer Pressure – I served on the staff of a church, directing orchestra for 37 years. There were at least a dozen on the staff.

When critical decisions came up, there was plenty of opportunity for agreement or dissent. There were times I found myself hesitating to state my view until I heard from others. Personality plays a role in this process. I'm told that my personality type is "Golden Retriever." That, in itself, would make me a little more hesitant to defend a position.

Fear – It often dictates what a person chooses to believe. I expect that some folks leaning over the rail of the Titanic, *chose* to believe in Heaven and a life hereafter out of fear for their final destiny.

Coercion – In many countries, people are forced to follow a religion which they don't agree with. If they refuse to comply, they are often abandoned by their families or, worse yet, their lives may be threatened for following a different religion.

Loyalty to Family Tradition – The most common reason for a person to choose a religion is because of strong cultural or family traditions. For example, in the Western hemisphere, Christianity is the common religion of most families.

Persons living in the Eastern Hemisphere more often have roots in Islam, Buddhism or the Hindu religion.

On the other hand, if a person's parents lean toward Agnosticism or Atheism, they may be more likely to follow that parental influence and less likely to follow the religion that is most common in their *culture* or hemisphere in which they live.

Media Bias – People of today's culture are very strongly influenced by the various media to which they are exposed. This is due in part to its fingertip availability, plus the great variety of media platforms. More than ever in history, the various media, such as television and computers, are so constantly available on a day-to-day if not hour-to-hour basis.

For that reason, there is the constant potential for such exposure to become a magnetic obsession.

- *The Social Media Craze – In 2004* Mark Zuckerberg, while in college, began developing his invention – Facebook. It started out as a simple, innocent effort to connect college kids sharing photos, stories and other personal information. In a very short span of time, it developed into a company whose product is really the people who use Facebook. Capitalizing on peoples innate emotions and natural instincts, it has developed into an enterprise which knows more about its users than their spouses do. It's a sophisticated information sponge and the information it accumulates is very valuable. Its success and formulas have linked it to many other sites. With 184 million users each day for almost an hour,[18] it's easy to estimate the impact on users who share family news, politics and yes ... even affect each other's beliefs.

- *Network Media Reporting* – The various popular news networks, largely controlled by wealthy individuals and large businesses, have evolved through the years, into news agencies which very often – perhaps most often – have liberal or conservative spins that reflect their political biases. Consequently, they are no longer broadcasting "news." Viewers, being creatures of habit, typically hear their news daily or nightly from the same voices. A relatively small proportion of viewers make use of more balanced news sources. But clearly, philosophical and religious viewpoints shared by the network media have a way of strongly affecting a person's beliefs and world views.

- *Higher Education* – Two or three decades ago, higher education had a strong reputation for promoting free speech. As with other forms of information, various pressures, political and otherwise, have affected their teaching in ways that don't allow the ideals of free expression to flourish as before. The topics which are taught have become very selective, reflecting the biases of its professors and upper leadership.

- That filtering process has syphoned its way into the high schools and has also trickled down into the elementary grades. Parents are often blind-sided by teachings they would not permit in a home-schooling environment. Private and religious schools, unfortunately, seem to remain the only option, especially in homes where both parents must work. This trend has significantly shaped religious beliefs, sexual practices, basic values and the world view of today's youth.

The media factors I have presented haven't impacted just today's youth but have had an ever increasing impact on all generations. Because many, if not most, of these media fail to offer a balanced perspective and fail to present both sides of the most critical issues, we may be totally unaware of the role they are playing in shaping the values and beliefs of both adults and children.

Quik Stop – C H A P T E R   F O U R T E E N

- What factors have influenced you the most in terms of the beliefs you hold today?   Peer pressure, Fear, Family Tradition, Media?

- When you develop an "opinion," on an issue, do you feel you are quite locked in, or capable of quite easily changing your mind once presented with evidence?

- Are you strongly locked in to a major "belief system" related to your faith or are you vascillating at this point?

- "Deists" believe in God as the Creator, but unlike Christians, they don't feel He interfaces with their lives as suggested in the first nine chapters. He simply leaves that to laws He has set in motion. If you believe there is a God, do you espouse the Deist view, the Christian view or some other view? Why?

- Are your values affected more by Conservative, Liberal or a balance of input sources?

- What forms of input play into your choices the most? For example: TV networks, social media (Facebook, Twitter etc.), dialog with friends, church, school.

C H A P T E R   1 5

Believe It or Not

We have wrestled with the most searching questions in the world: questions that have everything to do with the origins of the universe, a sovereign Creator-God, the origins of life, the formation of our beliefs, angels, and eternal destiny. This book is being read by *believers* who wish to strengthen their beliefs; by *agnostics* who are honestly searching for truth; and by *atheists* who opened the first chapter believing there is no God.

Some readers will close the book, leaving with the same beliefs that they may have clung to for years. Others may have raised the right questions but have never come face to face with the avalanche of fulfilled prophecy or the awesome proofs supporting the Resurrection. But for those who faced these facts head on, suddenly their entire belief system is shaken. Still others, whatever their theological persuasion, may simply be feeling an emptiness and a life lacking *purpose* and *relationship*.

Whichever of these positions comes closest to yours, this chapter may be the most important one you will ever read. As its author, I would not put you on a guilt trip. However, I would be the guilty one, if I failed to share what I know and have experienced. Someone once said, "Just tell me. Don't sell me." Having done so, I can relax knowing I have been honest with my readers by sharing what I personally believe to be the truth.

Thankfully, pursuing truth does not require a high I.Q. The Apostle Paul, a very intelligent, multi-lingual, eloquent philosopher in his own right, put his finger on a very striking irony: "God chose the foolish things of the world that he might confound those that are wise" (I Cor. 1:27 *KJV*). That truth has proven itself over and over. It is not my Ph.D. that qualifies me to ask or answer deep questions. Besides, there are theologians and scholars who are much more equipped than I, to scope out challenging theological issues.

The Case for Christ –

Allow me to introduce to you two highly intellectual men with remarkabl credentials. The first is Lee Strobel. For many years Lee has worked as an investigative reporter and attorney with the Chicago Tribune. In that role, he has encountered thousands of cases where his prowess as a researcher has gained him a strong reputation as a thorough, investigative journalist: one who looks through every possible window in search for truth.

Mrs. Strobel Throws a Curve – Lee's wife, an *agnostic*, one day informed him that she had become a Christian. The news hit him like a ton of bricks. Among the thoughts racing through his mind was the impact this could have on his reputation as a highly-respected attorney. But, beyond that, he honestly felt that she had somehow been tricked into a cult that had no foundation in reality. As a very brilliant scholar, he decided that he would research every source imaginable to prove to her the folly of her decision.

His journey, for two intense years, led him through all of the tests a criminal lawyer exploits to present a bullet-proof case. The trail led him to explore documentary evidence; eyewitness, scientific, psychological evidence; profile, medical, fingerprint evidence…and more. He scrutinized such subjects as messianic prophecy, ancient crucifixion methods, and Christ's Resurrection and post-resurrection appearances. Far more than an historical search, it included the evidence of cosmology, physics and biochemistry. And everything seemed to point in the direction of a Creator.

Those two intense years of research found him interrogating as many as fifteen experts in these various fields; reading all the liberal and atheistic literature; and standing in the shoes of skeptics, posing really tough questions. After all this, he became aware of a multitude of contradictions that didn't make sense. He knew that any researcher worth his salt has to arrive at some conclusion. In his words "… my biggest objection to Jesus had been quieted by the evidence of history. The great irony was this: it would require much more faith for me to maintain my atheism than to trust in Jesus of Nazareth."[19] One would do well to trace the details of his exhaustive journey in his book *The Case for Christ*.

The Most Convincing Evidence – If you've not read Lee's book, what might you think was the most convincing bit of evidence Strobel encountered in his extensive effort to disprove this "myth" of Christianity? The incredible, undeniable, statistical improbabilities surrounding the 100% fulfilled prophecies of Jesus, by themselves, would have been enough to drive a nail in the coffin of doubt. However, it all came down to the solidly convincing, unprecedented evidence for the Resurrection! Supported by the most reliable volley of *eye-witness accounts* any investigator could hope for.

While it is true that Christianity remains the religion with the largest following, I still haven't set up my domino string to offer you definitive proof that would lead to a satisfying conclusion. That will happen in the next chapter, so thanks for staying with me.

But meanwhile let me throw out some reasons some people don't become "believers" despite what seems to be very indisputable evidence. Could it be that human pride plays a role? Could it be that a person's attachment to the world or his or her habits and life-styles make one reluctant to adopt new beliefs? Might some individuals be embarrassed to follow a Person who was condemned and died as a common criminal?

We opened this book with a most insightful truism offered by a perceptive *atheist,* Antony Flew. He said, "Christians believe because they *want* to, but atheists don't believe because they *don't* want to."[20]

At the end of the day, discovering *truth* requires a tenacious, honest pursuit. If there is not that intense pursuit, it only proves the truth of the statement made by Flew.

It isn't really surprising that Lee Strobel became a Christian as a result of his search. Under the circumstances, we would suspect he started his search with a heavy bias. But the reality, I believe, is that anyone who pursues with an honest heart inevitably will discover this truth: "You will seek me and find me when you search for me with all your heart" (Jeremiah 29:13 *NAS*). Despite not being anxious to discover the validity of Scriptural Truth, Strobel was honest enough to concede the obvious.

Blended Beliefs –

Whether unaware of the evidence – or in spite of mountains of proofs - many people opt for a blended theology: a sort of mix and match approach. Thinking that *intelligence* probes the depths of life's deepest meanings, they take the best of Buddhism, Islam, and Hinduism, blended with some New Age and/or humanistic thinking, and hopefully stir in, vigorously, a bit of Christian doctrine in hopes of coming up with satisfactory answers for man's inner spiritual quests.

Something tells them that <u>more</u> is better. But everything we have learned about Christianity tells us that *less* is better.

In fact, any belief that acknowledges Jesus as Lord makes it clear that He is the *single*, exclusive path to life eternal. No words make this truth more clear than Jesus' own words when He said, "I am the only Way to God and the real Truth and the real Life; no one comes to the Father but through Me" (John 14:6 *AMP*).

Moses was a great leader. Abraham was father of a great nation. Paul was an awesome church leader. Other historic figures have founded great belief systems. So, you have a right to ask, "This being the case, what qualifies *Jesus* to be the solitary road to eternal life?"

Quite simply - and this is the pinnacle - the focal point of His Gospel: No one else has ever undergone a death quite as excruciating as crucifixion, then literally blown the door off His tomb and walked out unscathed!

For that very reason, alone, He is in a position to offer you and me something He also experienced Himself: *Eternal Life.*

This truth deserves a "Good Housekeeping Seal of Approval." The Resurrection stands alone! No non-scriptural belief system can be blended with the Resurrection.

Nor does the Resurrection need something else tacked onto it.

All roads may "lead to Rome," but *only one* road leads to eternal life.

Blending Judaism and Christianity – You have met Lee Strobel. Let me introduce you to *Louis Lapides*, a young man raised in a Jewish home. As part of a young man's bar mitzvah, or coming of age, they are required to do extensive study of the Jewish faith and the Hebrew language. Both Judaism and Christianity have the same roots; some of the same historic, great leaders; the very same lineage; and the same Biblical Commandments. If any two religions might be in harmony, it would be these two.

Lapides got his impressions of Jesus from reminders - seen in a Catholic church - of Christ's cross, crown of thorns and spilled blood. Judaism offered him beautiful ceremonies and traditions. But somehow Louis didn't feel like he had *a personal relationship with God*. With Judaism, it felt like, you got the rules. You lived by them, and that was that.

Lacking a personal connection, Lapides gravitated into Buddhism and Scientology. He said he probably accepted Satan's existence before God's.

One day, a Protestant pastor asked him, "Do you know of the *prophecy about the Messiah?*" (Prophecies, or the foretelling of Jesus, the Messiah are recognized by the Protestant faith but not by the Jewish faith.) Baffled by the words, he admitted to never even *hearing* about prophecy.

As the minister began to quote some prophecies from the Old Testament, Lapides thought, "Hey, these are verses from my own Jewish Scriptures he's quoting! How could *Jesus* be hiding in those chapters and verses?"

The pastor told him the Messiah came as Savior of the *whole* world, but that Christ originally came to Louis' own people.

Intrigued by all he was hearing, Lapides got alone with his Old Testament and, starting with Genesis, looked for Jesus in the sacred texts (written hundreds of years before they were fulfilled).

Who could this prophet be who was *"greater than Moses"* (Hebrews 3:3) and *had descended from his own Jewish lineage?*

With hesitance and trepidation, and against traditional advice, he finally went to the New Testament. There he found the genealogy of Abraham, Isaac and David (Matthew 1:1-6). In the opening verses, Matthew was quoting the words of a prophet (Matthew 1:23). How could Lapides have read in Isaiah about a "virgin who conceived and bore a son" and have totally missed this prophecy written 700 years before it happened (Isaiah 7:14)?

Even the Resurrection was blatantly obvious in the Psalmist's writing, suggesting that God "would not allow [HIS] Holy One to return to dust" (Psalm 16:10 NLV) but would ascend on high.

Lapides' skepticism was methodically eroding before his eyes. Is this why some rabbis discourage people from reading much of Isaiah? Does this explain synagogue seminars held to try to disprove the messianic prophecies?[21]

The more Lapides read, the more troubled he became. He realized that he would have to face up to the drugs, sex, and lifestyle he had accepted.

It was on a getaway in the Mojave Desert, with friends, when God so convincingly spoke to his heart. There, in that remote place, Louis spoke the words: "God, I accept Jesus into my life. I don't understand what I'm supposed to do with Him, but I want Him. I've pretty much made a mess of my life."[22]

From that point on, Louis was different. He observed, "...my friends knew my life had changed...All I know is that there's *someone* in my life...who's holy, who's righteous, who's a source of positive thoughts about life – and I just feel whole." [23]

What Louis discovered was not just a new system of beliefs and the intimate connection between the Old and New Testaments. He experienced a <u>*Personal Relationship with God*</u>. He realized this element was missing from the Theory of Evolution; since it leaves no one with whom to relate, *spiritually*. And the leaders of other great world religions are *incommunicado*. They've been gone for centuries. It is *relationship* that defines the Christian faith, because its founder, Jesus Christ, survived even the crucifixion...to offer us LIFE.

An interesting evolution in Louis' thinking had occurred. The more he read from those attempting to undermine evidence of Scriptural Truth, the more obvious became the flaws in their thinking.

There are many brilliant, educated Jews. Despite this fact, many of them have failed to come to even the most obvious conclusions summarized in this book.

But Messianic Christians abound.

Strobel tells the story of *Peter Greenspan*, an obstetrician-gynecologist and university professor, who had also been challenged to seek Jesus in Judaism. Troubled by what he had been hearing, he went to the Torah and Talmud. Like Lee Strobel, his motivation was to discredit Jesus' messianic credentials. However, his bottom line *conclusion* is *quite* revealing: "I think I actually came to faith in *Y'shua* by reading what detractors wrote."[24]

Atheism vs. Christianity –

These two belief systems have historically stood at painful odds. In Chapter One, I spoke of an historic debate where both sides met on a level playing field. The audience was the jury.

The historic faceoff occurred between Bill Craig in defense of Christianity, and Frank Zindler, an atheist spokesman selected by American Atheists, Inc. The crowd, including both Christian and Atheist numbered nearly 8,000 plus over 100 radio stations carrying the debate.

At the conclusion, ballots were circulated in the auditorium enabling individual response as to which position was the most compelling, apart from a debater's style or delivery. The reported results were not based on *number* of votes for either debater. (If Atheists outnumbered Christians, or vice versa, it would skew the results.)

Importantly, the results were based on a *percentage* of votes tallied for either Craig or Zindler respectively. Since the audience, upon entering the auditorium, had declared whether they were Atheist or Christian, it was possible to determine, for example, what percent of Christians considered Zindler's argument "most compelling" and similarly for Craig.

Significantly, an overwhelming 82% of "avowed atheists" concluded that "the case for Christianity was most compelling."

More significant is the fact that 45 persons entering as nonbelievers, indicated they were returning home as Christians, reversing their basic belief assumptions! In contrast, incidentally, "nobody became an atheist."[25]

As you've followed my journey and those of Strobel and Lapides, like some of the 45 persons referenced above, there may be something that's been gnawing away inside you – an emptiness and lack of relationship like Lapides described.

Many of the 45 above may have been sensing that same void and sense of hopelessness. What is it they are feeling? It's God's Holy Spirit nudging them – wanting to fill the void and replace it with His peace. You see, that's where *relationship* enters the picture. But maybe you're not totally convinced, thinking this may be just an emotional episode.

Good thinking. Because your decision needs to be above the shoulders. It must be based on factual evidence – one single event which is the entire basis of the Christian faith. I'm convinced it's what won the debate faceoff I just described. Read the next chapter and see if you believe the domino string holds up. If so, you may be ready to take the life-changing step, and you can then be sure it *isn't* an emotional whim.

"[If] you will seek the Lord your God, you will find Him if you seek Him with all your heart" (Deuteronomy 4:29, *NIV*).

Quik Stop – C H A P T E R   F I F T E E N

- Where do the beliefs of Christianity and Judaism blend together? Where do they part ways?
- In the historic Christianity vs. Atheism debate, what percent of Atheists felt Christianity was most compelling? 24%, 37%, 69%, 82%.
- For Lee Strobel, what body of truth was most compelling? The Resurrection or Prophecies surrounding the Messiah? Why?
- On a scale of 1 to 10, how compelling were the testimonies of Lee Strobel and Louis Lapides?

CHAPTER   SIXTEEN

Might the Domino String Collapse?

W hen I was a youngster, we had a box with at least 150 dominos which we would stand up in a long sequence.   To avoid the chain being knocked down prematurely, at some point we would carefully remove one domino to avoid setting off the chain. Still, it often happened that we not only set off a chain reaction but in both directions.

Like the string of dominos, if the *Resurrection* can be dispelled, then there is no credible reason to believe in *God,* nor *Jesus* nor *Heaven.* The whole domino string collapses. However, if one can demonstrate that Jesus really lived, died and rose from the dead, such a feat would be so incredible that anyone would be in total denial to suggest that His promises of a Heaven beyond are a mystical pipe dream. So it makes sense, to at least take a look at all the dominos in this chain.

1. *God* Is for Real

"Deism," is a belief system which, curiously, stands somewhere between Atheism and Christianity. Emerging in the 17th and 18th centuries, it presumes that God created all that exists, and that includes the physical laws that govern all of His creation.

But it assumes that He then stepped off of the stage of history and left creation to run on its own, propelled by natural law. Meanwhile, God is somewhere up in the ionosphere, kicking back in His Heavenly hammock. Thus, having no "relationship" with His creation. This implies that whatever happens in your life and mine is left to "fate" – pure chance. This, I think you know, is a *huge* distinction.

This book opened with almost a dozen stories, all suggesting that God is a central player on the stage of our lives. A God of "relationship." A God who loves us incredibly. This love is not a New Testament concept. It breathes through every Old Testament book as well.

In fact, every story in the book you are holding affirms God's passion to be a part of every detail of my life, whether a major career choice, or a fuel pump that's left me stranded in sub-zero Fargo, or which finds me lost on the other side of the world with only a dime in my pocket. Psalm 139 speaks of a God who knows when I'll sit or stand. A God who knows what I'll say before I say it. And if I take the winds to the far corners of the earth, there He is.

I will admit that a winning-streak of improbable stories doesn't offer definitive proof that God exists. But this next proof-positive pretty well drives a nail in the coffin of doubt.

2. *Jesus* Is for Real

Just as fingerprints and DNA are used to solve the many enigmas faced in court trials, there is a wealth of fingerprinting, that *unequivocally* confirms the existence of Jesus Christ. That evidence is found in "Biblical Prophecy" or *predictions* of future events.

Many prophecies relate to the rise and fall of kingdoms. However, the most impressive and most essential wealth of prophecy relates to *Jesus, the Messiah* – His birth, His life, His death and His Resurrection. There are at least four dozen *very* significant "messianic" prophecies scattered through the Bible. Incredible for their significance but also because they were accurately forecast *hundreds of years* before they actually happened!

If *any* of these prophecies should come to pass, it would be front page news because the statistical improbability is off the charts. But consider this stunning fact: Jesus, Himself, made the claim that <u>every</u> prophecy in *the entire Bible* concerning Himself *"must be fulfilled"* (Luke 24:44, *KJV*). The astonishing record?   Every prophecy, without exception, *has been fulfilled* – 100%!   Some statistician computed the astronomical odds based on just *eight* fulfilled prophecies.   The number is into the million billions.

Predicted Event	**Prophet**	**Approx. date of prophecy**
Born of a virgin	Isaiah 7:14	725 B.C.
Born in the town of Bethlehem	Micah 5:2	700 B.C.
Temporary sojourn in Egypt	Hosea 11:1	725 B.C.
From lineage of King David	Jeremiah 33:15	600 B.C.
Triumphal Entry on a Donkey	Zechariah 9:9	500 B.C.
Betrayal by a disciple	Psalm 41:9	1000 B.C.

Sold for 30 pieces of silver	Zechariah 11:13	500 B.C.
Method of his crucifixion	Isaiah 53:5	725 B.C.
Soldiers cast lots for his garments	Psalm 22:18	1000 B.C.
Legs not broken as was traditional	Psalm 34:20	1000 B.C.
Buried in a rich man's tomb	Isaiah 53:9	725 B.C.
Resurrection – He would NOT decay!	Psalm 16:10	1000 B.C.

Consider one of the most crystal-clear prophecies from the eloquent pen of Isaiah around 725 BC:

He was despised and rejected of men,
  A man of sorrows and acquainted with suffering.
He was pierced for our transgressions,
  He was crushed for our iniquities…
We all, like sheep, have gone astray …
  And the Lord has laid on Him the iniquity of us all.
He was led like a lamb to the slaughter
  And like a sheep before its shearers is silent
So He did not open His mouth.
  He was assigned a grave with the wicked,
And with the rich in his death,
  Though He had done no violence…
For He bore the sin of many,
  And made intercession for the transgressors."
(Selected verses from Isaiah 53, KJV)

Fifty years ago, I came upon a book that received much attention. It was titled *The Passover Plot* designed around the theory that Jesus and his disciples could have pre-arranged certain events that were clearly spelled out in the books of prophecy. The author, Hugh Schonfield offers a few examples: Entry into Jerusalem on a donkey – Sold for 30 pieces of silver – Buried in a rich man's tomb – Didn't open his mouth in self-defense. All of these events could have been pre-arranged.

But you can already anticipate some of the huge holes in this theory. How might they prearrange, by several hundred years, his ancestry or the city of His birth? Or especially His birth by a virgin? Or the method of His execution? Or the soldiers gambling for his garments? The last thing soldiers would be concerned about would be some prediction they didn't care a hoot about to begin with.

But listen to Schonfield's clincher: "We are nowhere claiming...that the book represents what actually happened."[26] The theory evaporates when he concedes that the Resurrection, following such a grueling crucifixion, would be extremely unlikely.

Unlikely? Call it IMPOSSIBLE! And that's precisely why the Resurrection occurred. It is the pivotal point on which the entire Christian faith is based! Then why go to the trouble of orchestrating a betrayal for 30 silver pieces – or the donkey entry – or borrowing a rich man's tomb? Rest assured. *Fulfilled prophecies are the most well-founded proofs* in the entire Jesus story apart from the Resurrection itself – which isn't the icing on the cake. It *is* the cake!!

3. The *Resurrection* Is for Real
The one single distinguishing feature of the Christian faith

is the fact of *the Resurrection* – the last domino standing! Anyone with the slightest inclination to think Jesus might have somehow survived the torture of the cross, may read the gory details from a number of sources. Alexander Metherell, M.D., Ph.D. has the medical and scientific credentials to detail Jesus' execution.[27] Survival from Friday night to Sunday morning is beyond the remotest possibility. This alone makes the Resurrection a fact we can hang our hats on.

Despite this fact, D.A.s needed some *story*. So they fabricated the rumor that there was no Resurrection, insisting that his body was stolen.

But God, in His infinite wisdom, wisely foiled that rumor by arranging Jesus' Resurrection appearances from Jerusalem to the north shores of Galilee.

These were not flash-in-the pan sightings. No look-alikes. No mystical semi-transparent, elusive figures. No distant, fleeting "Big Foot"-style glimpses leaving us to question whether it was a mirage or the real thing.

Nor were His appearances a quick drop-in, drop-out scenario. For six or seven long weeks He continued to join strangers for lunch; probably picked up a few dinner tabs; met casual acquaintances at their workplace, or a few disciples for a Starbucks latte. The string of sightings was so extensive that denying His reappearance would be the height of misguided conjecture. The list reads like a "Who's Who in the Holy Land."

- Mary Magdalene (John 20:10-18)
- The other women at the tomb (Matthew 28:8-10)
- Cleopas and another disciple en route to Emmaus (Luke 24:13-32)

- Eleven disciples and others (Luke 24: 33-19)
- Ten apostles and others, minus Thomas (John 20:19-23)
- Thomas and the other apostles (John 20:26-30)
- Seven apostles (John 21:1-14)
- Some apostles at the Mount of Olives before His ascension (Acts 1:4-9)
- *A crowd of 500* in one setting (I Corinthians 15:6)

It was Paul who reported the 500 eye witnesses. And it's estimated that some 10,000 more became followers on the heels of the reports by fired up eye witnesses.

And yes, this was the very Apostle Paul, once a serial killer of Jesus' followers, whom God struck blind while en route to kill another large contingency in Damascus. That singular incident made Paul a "never-say-die" believer who launched the largest following of any religion in history: 2.3 *billion* Jesus-followers as of this date!

4. *Heaven* Is for Real

We've covered a lot of ground since Chapter One. Thanks for staying with me because we've saved the dessert for last.

One of the most anticipated promises came from the lips of Jesus Himself. Before He left this planet, He left us with these reassuring words: "I go to prepare a place for you" (John 14: 2 *NAS*). And you can take that promise to the bank! Knowing His prophetic promises have a 100% fulfillment record, why would we wonder at the likelihood of His fulfilling *this* promise? Like all the proofs in our string of dominos, God totally covered this base as well.

The Apostle John left us with a very vivid description of what we can expect Heaven to look like. In addition, I'm convinced that, in these last days, God's "Master Plan" to give certain people, a brief glimpse of the other side of Heaven's gates, isn't just for their own personal edification. Like Paul and John, their sojourn confirms, without contradiction, that Heaven is a very <u>real</u> place. Their testimony is fresh and provides an added confirmation of John's timeless words.

The splendor and expanse of Heaven consists of three virtually indescribable parts of God's creation: The *Throne Room* of God, The *City* of God (or "New Jerusalem), and *Paradise*. Let's join the Apostle John as he takes us on the grand tour.

The Apostle John's View of Heaven –

Anyone who has visited India's Taj Mahal stands astonished beyond belief. As one of the "New Seven Wonders," it is considered the architectural jewel of the planet."

But there is a structure that, by far, supersedes any other. Situated at the very peak of the "City of God," it has been described as the most magnificent and impressive structure in the entire universe housing the most powerful Person in all of the *Universe*: *God, the Creator.*

Some may ask, "Who is this John?" *The Apostle John* was one of the 12 disciples who followed Jesus while He was on earth. He was eventually imprisoned on the Mediterranean Isle of Patmos while writing the book of Revelation, which describes, in detail, much of Heaven. What can we expect of destination-Heaven? We may discover that the anticipated Heaven experience will include exotic explorations of the vast expanses of the Universe. Why not?

Rachel and I visited the confined space on that island – really, a cave – in which John penned the entire book. The vast, expansive Mediterranean Sea glistening below, was truly knock-out impressive. But when John wrote about a new heaven and a new earth where "there was no longer any sea" (Rev. 21:1 *NIV*), he may have seen this vast Mediterranean as a prison wall from which he could not escape. That is, until the day he was taken up and ushered by an angel into the portals of Heaven.

The Throne Room –

Try to picture the *"Throne Room* of God" at the apex/pinnacle of God's creation. Everything, including the "City of God" and "Paradise," stands below it. John describes in detail some of the glories we will relish when *we* get to Heaven's portal.

He doesn't go into great detail describing the Throne Room itself; perhaps because nothing in all of Heaven could be more 'indescribable.' He was probably speechless. Like typing a novel with only half of the keys. But the Throne Room is the residence from which God rules this mighty universe.

If my description sounds too literal, get used to it. Heaven, from John's pen and the testimony of others who have been privileged to see it, is more *real* than the book you are holding!

Heaven's Music – As a musician, there's a scene surrounding the Throne of God that I anticipate more than any other. I can hardly wait to experience it. John speaks of continuous songs of praise to the Almighty by "thousands of thousands" of voices (Rev. 5:11 *NASB)* converging on "a huge sea of glass" *surrounding* the Throne Room. Most others, like Heaven visitor Patrick Doucette, spoke of more than music, when he recalled a center of art, worship, dance and creativity "in a large oval area" sparkling like … "sapphire jewels."[28]   Airline Captain Dale Black, like Apostles John and Paul, reported "flying in" with angels. It seems to be the primary mode of transportation.

Already very familiar with sky views, Dale estimated this crystal worship platform at over ten miles diameter.[29]   The many similar, ecstatic but varied accounts are clearly not copy-cats but faithfully lend additional appreciation and color to what John was recalling.

What one described as a "massive arena, charged with an energy beyond comprehension"[30] John also recalled. "*Every created thing*, both in Heaven and Earth, made their voices heard, *simultaneously*, singing, 'To Him…be blessing and honor, glory and dominion forever and ever' (Rev. 5:13 *NASB*)." How awe-inspiring that massive sound had to be!!

The City of God –

John spent much more time detailing "The *City* of God," which John also called the "New Jerusalem" just _below_ the Throne Room. The "River of Life" is described as flowing "into and out of" the Throne Room and then down through the great golden street of the city. On each side is "The Tree of Life," which, each month, blossoms with a different fruit.

John described this city on a great high mountain as if it were some transcendental space odyssey experience. Its brilliance, like "…a stone of crystal-clear jasper" (Rev. 21:11 *NASB*) couldn't be exaggerated; it had "no need of the sun or the moon … for its lamp is the Lamb," (Rev. 21:23 *NASB*) the Son of God. Even from a distance its brightness had to be mind-blowing.

John's Description – Figurative or Literal? – First of all, let's shed our *small world* mentality. Thinking back on the cave we visited on the Isle of Patmos, it's no surprise that everything John saw staggered his imagination. A cell cam would quickly run out of memory. John's senses were so full throttle that his angel-host had to measure every colossal dimension.

A Perfect Cube – Most impressive had to be *the huge, gargantuan size and shape* of this city – a perfect cube, *1,400 miles in all three directions* as measured by the angel. I'm humored that, like a little kid, he asked his host to whip out the tape measure again. "Just dig the *thickness* of these gigantic walls!" Would this request make sense if the city was not literal? The walls measured an unimaginable 216-feet thick by *human* measurements, "which are also _angelic_ measurements" (Revelations 21:17 *NASB*). Perhaps a bit of John's dry humor coming out. His point? This city is *very* huge...and _very, very real_. I'll let you engineers confirm the need for a wall this thick.

I wondered if this city was designed to accommodate all of the believers of the ages. Let's see, 1,960,000 square miles. That's 1/3 the land mass of the U.S. But a wall 1,400 miles high? I thought "what a huge waste of space." But wait. This is "gravity-free" territory. Including the top and sides, that's almost 12 million square miles of regal real estate! And some have speculated the city could have layers. Why not, since travel is at the speed of thought! That would allow 2 ¾ *billion* cubic miles to work with. Let's just know that God has a handle on the space requirements.

Some added detail caught John's eye. Each of the gates was made of a single pearl! Who wouldn't be impressed with that?

We already know the streets were "pure gold, like transparent glass" (Rev. 21:21 *NASB*). NASA scientists tell us that when ALL impurities are removed from gold, you can see through it. In fact, the city itself was of pure, *transparent* gold.

But there are four things the city did *not* possess. *First*, there was no temple. God's word says, "...the Lord God...and the Lamb, are its temple" (Rev. 21:22 *NASB*.) *Second*, there was "...no night there and its gates will never be closed" (Rev. 21:25 *NASB*.) *Third*, there will be " no more death ... mourning, or crying, or pain" (Rev. 21:4). Best of all, the security system: "Nothing unclean …will ever come into it, but only those whose names are written in the Lamb's book of life" (Rev. 21:27 *NASB*.)

Paradise –

A city-slicker from New York City may never have seen beyond his concrete prison. He may have never seen a real cow. But hang on. Heaven can't be less than this world!

That's what Paradise is all about. It surrounds the "City of God." John didn't (probably couldn't) describe Paradise. When Apostle Paul was caught up into Paradise, he was forbidden to talk about "inexpressible things…that man is not permitted to tell (II Corinthians 12:4)." Why is that? Perhaps any description would downplay its reality and beauty by a factor of 1,000 to 1. Now, that reason I can buy.

One clue we have, however, is that Heaven, also described as the "New Earth," will possess the features of *this* earth including the animals and aquatic life we now enjoy. That implies their survival habitat – lakes, streams, foliage, mountains. God has made it clear that He is not *replacing* everything; rather He is making "*all things* new" (Matthew 19:28). I believe that means music, art, food, laughter; everything we treasure. Some have claimed to have seen grass and flowers so absolutely perfect in every detail; effervescent with thousands of colors never seen on this planet.

Suffice it to say, ANYTHING we experience in Heaven will be exponentially greater than what we can think or imagine. Why would we expect less, given the resources of His creative genius? Do you understand why I hesitate to attempt any further description of the indescribable?

This Author's Perspective –

Nothing in this entire book (and that includes this chapter) in any way *contradicts* the testimony you have just read from the Apostle John as it relates to bottom-line truth and basic beliefs. But some have this fear that Heaven will be so UNREAL … so cosmic and ethereal that they want nothing to do with it. For all the shortcomings of John's vision and vocabulary, what he wanted most to get across is this: "Heaven is VERY REAL." You can count on it.

As I write, I glance out my window and see bicyclists cruising by while wearing masks. In every store, masks are part of the required apparel right now. The COVID-19 pandemic gives one the sense we might be on a new or different planet.

I flip on the news and, night after night, witness major cities being trashed and pummeled by terrorists: looting, killing and unprecedented vandalism. It's the most preposterous scene I've witnessed in my life.

There is more antagonism and bitter hatred in politics than we have seen in all our nation's history. Faith in our government has dwindled. And this is *reality*? Is this the new normal? It's more like watching the old vintage, black/white, cathode-ray TV, fuzzy and flickering out of control. I'll take today's brilliant, hi-res, 72" LCD …boasting millions of colors.

The Real Me – God's Word tells us of an inner longing that won't be satisfied until we experience Heaven – the *ultimate* reality. To some extent, we are all uncomfortable with our earthly shell. Who defines who I am? What I'm worth? Whether I'm "failing" or "succeeding"? My ultimate purpose?

The chatter at my first high school class reunion revolved around peoples' jobs; their recent promotions; their nice, new yachts. "One-upsmanship" was a subtle but familiar game. If you've experienced similar moments, in your heart you sensed you weren't talking to the "real person." Just the one he or she would *like* to be.

Let's face it. We are, in varying degrees, affected by others' approval: what our neighbors think about our chosen profession; how our lawn measures up to others' lawns; or whether our old car comes up to some unspoken standard. Possessions and a nest egg for security dictate "success" in "the game of life." The one with the most toys wins.

Now Imagine Heaven – where suddenly there is no pressure, no pretense, no insecurity, no jealousy, no distrust, no comparison-making, no sense of failure, and no anxiety. No worries whatsoever. Now *that's* "real!" Love for everyone in our forever circle is so incredibly powerful and mutual that nothing else matters. Even making God happy is as natural as breathing. Being totally "myself" will be one of the great serendipities of that final destination. Wow!

Leaving the Throne Room –

In my mind's eye, I imagined a scene from the Bible. Two thousand years ago Jesus and God, the Father - two "Persons" of the Trinity - met together in this very Throne Room. It was an encounter that would change the course of history. The human race had so obviously and miserably failed to reflect any true comprehension of God's Love. A shortcoming of ours – not His. To most mortals, "God" seemed an impersonal figure propped up on an unreachable pedestal.

To cross this great hurdle and demonstrate the warmth and personal touch of God's Love, His only Son would have to leave the throne of Heaven, be born in a cavern's stable, take on an incarnate form, and live among men while demonstrating the most supreme example of Love.

It would be here, in Heaven's Throne Room, that Jesus agreed to wrap Himself in human flesh and subject Himself to unbelievable ridicule and excruciating pain. Willingly He would lay down his life, demonstrating, once and for all, a Love that could be conveyed in no other way than a death worse than that suffered by any criminal on a cross. This story is so well portrayed through the Scriptures that it needs no further amplification. Nor could it ever be repeated.

Quik Stop – C H A P T E R   S I X T E E N

- What belief system straddles the fence between Christianity and Atheism?
- What serial killer did God appoint to launch a world-wide movement and what event turned his life around?
- Which of the predicted events in the "Jesus Is For Real" graph, was the real clincher when it comes to establishing the 2,000-year legacy of Christianity?
- What percent of prophecies related to Jesus have been fulfilled? 37%, 58%, 98%, 100%
- How compelling, for you, were each of the four realities presented in this chapter: God, Jesus Christ, the Resurrection and Heaven?
- When you finished reading this chapter, were the four dominos still standing? If not, which was, or were, not?
- **If they are still standing, can you find yourself believing because you *want* to believe?**

C H A P T E R   S E V E N T E E N

Heaven Is Really for Real

B y now you know that there are *three* areas of experience that, collectively, validate all that I believe about Heaven.

First of all, half of this book has been about *improbabilities* in my life: occurrences that, from a purely statistical perspective, were so absolutely remote that they could not likely have occurred without a God-Presence.

A *second,* much more convincing window was the stunning 100% *fulfilled prophecies* related to Jesus' birth, life and death.

The *third,* the most important window, is the Resurrection. And that domino is still standing!

What is a "Believer"? –

The common word referring to a Christian is "believer." But to avoid confusion, let's clarify what the term means.

In terms of intellectual assent, you may be quite convinced of the Scriptures' Truth. But being convinced in your head doesn't make you a "believer." We cited the classic example in Acts 26:28. King Agrippa was teetering on the brink of decision but concluded "You've *almost* persuaded me to be a Christian" (Acts 26:28 my paraphrase). What prevented him from throwing his hat in the ring 100%? A need to be in control? Peer pressure? Perhaps a resistance to acknowledging the sin in his life. Maybe pride which holds millions of people back.

So what *does* qualify a person as a true "believer?" The answer is so simple that, as Isaiah wrote, "not even a fool can misunderstand it." (Isaiah 35:8 *my paraphrase*)

1)   <u>Recognize</u> you are a sinner in need of a Savior.

2)   <u>Repent</u> of your sins, and turn from your selfish ways.

3)   <u>Accept</u> the free gift of salvation, purchased by Jesus' death on the cross.

This simple plan deserves a few helpful comments.

•   The plan is FREE. Compare with any other religion where you earn salvation by *doing good works*. With Christianity, the "doing" was accomplished when Jesus died on the cross. While works naturally follow out of love, you can't possibly earn it. Salvation, pure and simple, is His "gift" to us.

•   The plan is SIMPLE. Too simple? The *Greek word* for *"repent"* means *turning 180 degrees - reversing the direction* of your life. You become a true *"disciple"* (literally *"learner"*) of Jesus.

•   The plan includes GRACE for your entire journey. You will stumble ... you'll fall. Return to where you fell and claim His grace. It's available today... tomorrow... and forever.

- This plan is the ONLY way to Heaven. A common belief is that there are many ways to God. But Jesus insisted, "I am the Way and the Truth and the Life. No one comes to the Father except through Me (John 14:6 *NIV*).

- This plan is NOT EXCLUSIVE. However deep the hole you've dug, "*all* have sinned and fall short of the glory of God" (Romans 3:23 *NAS*). You can't live long enough to be worthy. Consider the thief hanging on the cross beside Jesus. His clock was at 12 midnight when Jesus assured him of "Paradise." Or consider Apostle Paul; a serial killer. "God so loved the world that He gave His only begotten Son, that whosoever believes in Him shall not perish but have eternal life" (John 3:16 *KJV*).

Two suggestions while joining the ranks of the Believers:

- <u>Don't overcomplicate it</u> by thinking you can earn it.
- <u>Don't oversimplify it</u>, assuming there need be no change in your life.

You are about to embark on the most exciting, rewarding journey you can imagine. You'll find that it *is* life-changing. Not because you *have* to change your life but because you *want* to.

Are we on board so far? Your next question may be, "What if I don't decide either way?" The answer is simple: *Indecision* means that *you've already decided.*

I very well remember someone speaking on this subject. He posed a very pragmatic response to anyone in the audience who was unwilling to make the choice to follow Jesus. He said, "My eternal destiny and yours hang in the balance. One of us is right; one of us is wrong. If I am wrong, there is no eternal consequence. But what if you are wrong? What then?"

Moment of Decision – No words are adequate to explain the "conversion" experience. It's a *Personal Relationship with God* which Louis Lapides discovered (see the end of Chapter 15).

These thoughts very well summarize my personal experience:

> I'm a "Skeptic" by nature. I was born with it.
> I'm a "Believer" by evidence. I can't deny it.
> I'm a "Follower" by choice. I can't help it.

If you have decided to make this your decisive moment, I would invite you to offer a prayer of confession and become a believer/receiver. You may either pray in your own words, or you can pray the prayer below. Either way, I would urge you to make it *audible*. There is something about verbalizing a request that makes it more indelible in one's mind.

"Dear Jesus, I come to You **recognizing my sin** and knowing that I need a Savior. I thank You for the great sacrifice You made by dying on the Cross.

I repent of my sins and trust You for complete forgiveness. As a born-again believer, I recognize that You are the Way, the Truth and the Life;

I accept Your free gift of Eternal Life and I commit all I am and have to you. I now can pray 'in Jesus' name.' Amen."

Because this experience is the start of a brand new life, Jesus referred to it as being "born again." You can now celebrate *two* "birthdays." (In that case, you may even wish to jot down the date of your new birth: _____.)

Welcome to the growing Family of Believers!

Quik Stop – C H A P T E R   S E V E N T E E N

How can I learn to share what I've just experienced?
If you have just begun your walk of faith as a new believer, you will want to share that new-found faith with someone. It may be your spouse or a roommate. Perhaps a co-worker on the job.

It's part of growing and maturing in your new faith. Start while the experience is fresh. Your friends should see something different in you as there was in Lapides.

God uses each of us in different ways. Some are gifted to just *plant seeds* along the path. Some are comfortable with *watering those seeds* with, perhaps, brief comments during water-fountain chats. Others are blessed with the ability to *harvest the seed*, perhaps through some counseling opportunities.

Here are some ways you can begin to share in a way that fits your personality:

- You might start by sharing your concise story with us. What has happened? You may contact us at: JerryNelsonMusic.com
- Get your hands on a Bible. A very readable version is the Life Application Study Bible, NLT – New Living Translation, and begin reading in John; then progress on to James.
- Find a Bible based church and join believers in a Bible study.
- Ask God to open a door to share with someone. When it swings open, don't barge in. Ease in and let God be

your coach. Then consider sharing with us that experience so we can join in praying with you.

- You may know someone who is confused, desperate, marriage on the brink, jobless, suicidal or far from God; but you feel totally unprepared to counsel them through. If you feel gifting a book like this could open their heart *and do the speaking for you*, read about "**Gift-a-Book**" in the back pages of this book. It's our way of partnering with you as you share your journey with others.

Jerry's music career has touched millions on all continents through global TV and over 1,000 concerts.

As a musician, Jerry performs as a soloist. But he'd be the first to say he couldn't do it without Rachel's hard work and support. Together they make an extraordinary team. Their prayer is that their journey will link up with yours; if not on this planet – then in Heaven!

NOTES

Chapter 1 – Is Heaven Really for Real?

[1] Todd Burpo, *Heaven is for Real.* (Nashville, TN, Thomas Nelson Inc. © 2010 by Todd Burpo).

[2] From "Mountain Rhapsodies," a piano / orchestral project featuring Classical, Hebraic and Broadway pieces including "Titanica." Recorded at Eagles Nest Recording Studios – Conifer, Colorado (JerryNelsonMusic.com) #J1013.

"Titanica" also appears on the recording "Is Heaven Really For Real?" You may wish to listen to the "Titanica" recording with an ear to these musical cues which guide you through a blow-by-blow narrative of *Titanic's journey* from its launching to its demise:

- 0:01   *Love Theme* (Bagpipe = the Gentleman; Ulan pipes = the Lady)

- 0:20   *Boarding Ship* (Fog Horns - Bassoon with Low Brass)

- 0:34   *Christening Fanfare and Launch* (Trumpets)

- 1:10   *Out to Sea* (Choral, Soaring strings, Pulsating Piano & Lo Strings = throbbing sound of engines and splashing ocean waves)

- 2:25   *Festive Dancing* (Strauss waltzes. "Blue Danube" one of the hits of the day)

- 3:33   1st *Quiet Nights Theme* (Pno, Fl, Stgs marking the 1st of 3 nights at sea)

- 4:46   *Saturday night dance* (Tpt, Tbn, Clar. play popular Ragtime hits)

- 5:50   2nd *Quiet Nights Theme* (Pno, Fl Stgs marking 2d night of voyage)

- 7:00   *Sunday AM Worship led by Captain Smith* (Horn & Voices – familiar hymns)

- 8:45   *Tales from Vienna Woods* (Music only - Dancing not allowed on Sunday)

- 9:33   *Ice warnings from ship 'Californian'* (Xylophone = Morse code interrupting the orchestra music)

- 9:54   *Titanic operators rude response* (Piano plays an irritating flurry of notes)

- 10:12   *3d Quiet Nights Theme* (Flute introduces the final, fatal quiet night)

- 10:31   *Final ice warnings* (Xylophone = 'Californian' with Piano = Irritated Titanic Morse code response)

- 10:53   *Titanic approaches iceberg at 23 knots* (Piano, ugly chords)

- 11:00   *Iceberg tears open five compartments, Suspense* (Tremolo strings)

- 11:04   *High alert Signal* (Three successive bell sounds)

- 11:17   *Water penetrating ship* (Descending Piano and Strings, Ship's builder inspecting damage)

- 11:40   *Water penetrates lower cabins* (Piano and rude, low brass)

- 12:00+   *Water level rapidly rising in ship* (rising string tremolo, brass, agitated piano)

- 12:55+   *Bow of ship sinking, Stern heaves high in the air for almost 60 seconds, before ripping loose of the bow and plunging down 2 ½ miles* (Heavy brass descending chords)

- 13:38   *Middle of night, 710 survivors float in lifeboats* (Quiet woodwinds)

- 14:05   *Ship and 1,514 passengers have disappeared* (A lifeboat survivor begins "Nearer, My God to Thee" joined gradually by others until singing fades away)

- 15:36   *Love Theme* (Bagpipe – Gentleman; Ulan pipe – Lady. Both bobbing in 28-degree freezing water while clinging to a floating board. The gentleman yields the board to his lover as the Bagpipe sound disappears; Ulan Pipe sounds the last dying phrase.)

[3] Wikipedia, **Sinking of the Titanic – Details:** • 883' long, 104' high, 52,300 tons displacement • 29 coal furnaces, 600 tons/day hand-shoveled • A 300-ft. stretch incurred several openings up to 39 ft • Sinking after 2hr, 40min • Eventual displacement = 35,000 tons of water • Women & children boarded lifeboats first • 1,514 (68%) lost / 710 saved • Lifeboat capacity 1,200+ • Only 13 rescued in water by lifeboats • Bow & stern ripped in half; descended 12,451 ft at 25-30 mph for 5+ minutes • Stern section cratered 49 feet in

sand • Passenger list (lost) included Millionaire John Jacob Astor, Macy's owner Isidor Straus and Titanic designer Thomas Andrews • (saved) Molly Brown – Eliza Gladys Dean, on lifeboat at 2 months; last survivor, she died at 97. • *Titanic* was discovered 73 years later • Visits to wreckage starting in 2021- $125,000 per person plus assisting as part of the crew on discoveries to build a scale facsimile. (https://en.wikipedia.org/wiki/Sinking_of_the_Titanic).

[4] Lee Strobel, *The Case for Christ* (Zondervan Publishing House, Grand Rapids, MI. Copyright © 1998 by Lee Strobel), 239.

Chapter 10 – Angels in Disguise

[5] The "Herald of Holiness" is a monthly publication of the Church of the Nazarene.

Chapter 11 – Out of This World

[6] Todd Burpo, *Heaven Is For Real.* (Nashville, TN, Thomas Nelson Inc. © 2010 by Todd Burpo), 63.

[7] Ibid. 86.

[8] Ibid. 93-96.

[9] Ibid. 145.

[10] Glenn Beck's interview with Akiane on CNN. https://www.historyvshollywood.com/video/akiane-kramarik-cnn-interview/

[11] Akiane Kramerik, *Painting the Impossible* (YouTube video), https://www.youtube.com/watch?v=Wm9BGxpf0hU

[12] Michael H Hart, *The 100: A Ranking of the Most Influential Persons In History*. Time Magazine. (First published in 1999, new editions of this book are released each year; recent editions ranking only living persons).

Chapter 12 – Devil's Advocate

[13] Billy Graham, *Facing Death* (Waco, TX, Word Books. © 1987 by Billy Graham), 35.

[14] Randy Alcorn, *Heaven* (Tyndale House Publishers, Inc., Carol Stream, IL. Copyright ©2004 by Eternal Perspective Ministries), 5.

[15] Billy Graham, 39.

[16] Richard Sigmund, *My Time in Heaven* (Whitaker House, New Kensington, PA. Copyright © 2004, 2010 by Cleft of the Rock Ministries), 34, 35.

Chapter 13 – When Does Life Really Begin?

[17] Todd Burpo, 94, 95.

Chapter 14 – Beliefs Aren't Born in a Vacuum

[18] Tucker Carlson, *Ship of Fools* (New York, N.Y., Simon and Schuster, Inc. Copyright © 2018 by Tucker Carlson), 41.

Chapter 15 – Believe It Or Not

[19] Lee Strobel, *The Case For Christ* (Zondervan Publishing House, Grand Rapids, MI. Copyright ©1998 by Lee Strobel), 265.

[20] Ibid. 239.

[21] Ibid. 182.

[22] Ibid. 180.

[23] Ibid. 181.

[24] Ibid. 186.

[25] Ibid. 206.   For a tape of the debate, see William Lane Craig and Frank Zindler, *Atheism vs. Christianity: Where Does the Evidence Point?* (Grand Rapids: Zondervan, 1993), video.
The debate may also be viewed on YouTube:
https://www.youtube.com/watch?v=HuCA4rIX4cE

Chapter 16 – Might the Domino String Collapse?

[26] Lee Strobel, *The Case For Christ* (Zondervan Publishing House, Grand Rapids, MI. Copyright ©1998 by Lee Strobel), 192.

[27] Ibid. 194-204.

[28] John Burke, *Imagine Heaven* (Baker Books, Grand Rapids, MI. Copyright ©2015 by John Burke), 313.

[29] Ibid. 314.

[30] Ibid. 313.

□   □   □   □   □

If this book had a meaningful impact on your view
of God or Heaven – if you found it inspirational or
changed your life in some significant way, there are a
couple of things you could do to share your
experience with others:

• Visit Amazon.com; search for this book and **leave
a review**
• Share this resource on any of your **social media**
pages

Your review could make all the difference in
someone's life.

Jerry Nelson – Musician / Entrepreneur

 Jerry Nelson is a thought provoking story teller – through words as well as notes. His career has taken him to all continents, as Concert Pianist, Recording Artist and Conductor of orchestras from Los Angeles to London and Tel Aviv. While composing original songs, his strongest suit has resulted in some 6,000 musical arrangements – and all of this while directing music at Denver First Church for 37 years.

Jerry's entrepreneurial pursuits found him and his sons, Scott and Brad, building Eagles Nest Studio on a mountain peak in Colorado – a four-year venture into most of the building trades. Inspired by a 12,000 square-mile view, hundreds of artist projects were recorded on this pinnacle.

His entrepreneurial bent also showed up when he spear-headed the Performance Tracks industry. Somewhat like Karaoke for schools, churches and solo artists, performance tracks are now used to accompany artists world-wide.

Jerry has kept a 60-year journal of personal events for which he finds no explanation other than an indisputable God-presence. These stories with "unequivocal" Biblical proofs, resulted in a book that points people of all faiths – or no faith – toward a loving God whose passion is a very personal relationship with the creatures of His creation.

Gift-a-Book to someone ...
and we'll gift the Recording!

Who do you know that ...

... has **given up hope** and maybe **giving up on life**?
... is a **grandson** or **daughter** that's taken the low road?
... is in **hospice** and could use a lift?
... is **jobless** and sees **no future**?
... is in the **military** or overseas?
... has a **birthday** coming up?
... would enjoy this book for **Christmas**?
... maybe isn't ready for **Heaven**?

Is Heaven Really For Real? could be the lift they need ... or could show them the "free"way to Heaven.

Let us partner with you in reaching them.

You *gift*
this book

We will *gift*
this **FREE** CD

How to Secure the FREE CD

If you have purchased your *personal* **book and music recording** (scout's honor), for each book you **gift**, you will receive the **FREE, double-length** companion **CD**.

Go to our website: **JerryNelsonMusic.com**, and place an order for your **Gift-A-Book** package(s). Need help ordering? Ask a younger relative to assist you.

Q: **When can I take advantage of this offer?**
A: Anytime!

Q: **How often can I place an order?**
A: As often as you wish!

Q: **What is the limit on quantity?**
A: There is NO quantity limit!

Visit **www.JerryNelsonMusic.com** to *Gift-a-Book*.

This is our way of partnering with you as you reach out to friends who need your touch.

Jerry's Fully Orchestrated Piano Music
... available in a wide variety of styles

CDs and DVDs

Jerry's creatively arranged and
performed piano CDs and DVDs include
a broad selection of genres:

Sacred
Classical
Jazz
Celtic
Quiet Piano-Only Hymns
Gospel
Broadway Hits
Christmas
Inspiring Heaven Songs
and more!

28 to choose from!

heet Music & ccompaniment Tracks

ten to full demos of Jerry Nelson's unique, ginal arrangements of your favorite songs d purchase sheet music for Piano, Solo struments, Orchestra, Big Band, and Vocal. mpanion Performance/Accompaniment cks available.

so, FREE products!

ne Voice Hymnal Products

mns for the people of God. This new hymnal ntains 234 songs and 93 inspirational readings r personal devotion and corporate worship. e 12-CD set (or USB drive) is a recording of the TIRE hymnal with piano by Jerry Nelson, mass oir, and organ. *Also available in split track rmat and Accompaniment Book.*

USB card for car or computer

Heaven Really For Real?
What are the Odds?

ok and CD available individually, as a set, or with e Gift-A-Book option (see Amazon for ebook)

Visit **JerryNelsonMusic.com**
to place an order or request additional information

A portion of the proceeds from all purchases will be applied to our mission and humanitarian efforts in Rwanda and DRC Congo.

World Wide Connections | WWConnections.org